NO MORE EGGSHELLS

A Practical Guide To Understanding, Coping And Living With Someone Who Has Borderline Personality Disorder Or Narcissistic Personality Disorder

I. Madison

FREE BONUS INSIDE

3rd Edition

© **2016 Copyright.**

Text copyright reserved. I. Madison

The contents of this book may not be reproduced, duplicated or transmitted without direct written permission from the author

Disclaimer : All attempts have been made by the author to provide factual and accurate content. No responsibility will be taken by the author for any damages caused by misuse of the content described in this book. The content of this book has been derived from various sources. Please consult a licensed professional before attempting any techniques outlined in this book.

Table of Contents

Introduction 4

Chapter 1: Narcissism and BPD: What are these Conditions? 6

Chapter 2: How Can You Tell a Narcissist When Courting? 10

Chapter 3: How to Identify Narcissists at Your Workplace 14

Chapter 4: Narcissism from a Religious Perspective 19

Chapter 5: Where to Begin 26

Chapter 6: How Narcissism Varies From BPD 30

Chapter 7: Strategies for Living with a Narcissist 37

Chapter 8: How to End Manipulation by a Narcissist 41

Chapter 9: Strategies for Living with someone who has BPD 49

Chapter 10: How To Keep Sane When Your Loved One Has BPD 54

Chapter 11: Communicate and Behave As Differently As the Person with BPD 58

Chapter 12: How to Handle an Employee with BPD 64

Chapter 13: Simple Changes for a Happier Life 71

Chapter 14: Anything Good You Can Reap From The Narcissist? 74

Chapter 15: Handling a Narcissist without Losing Control of Your Emotions 79

Chapter 16: Treatment for People with BPD 85

Chapter 17: Tips for a Family with a Person with BPD 89

Conclusion 109

BONUS 110

Introduction

Whether you've noticed it yourself or it's been pointed out to you by someone who's concerned, you may find yourself reading this guide because you or a loved one is involved in a relationship with a narcissist or an individual who has borderline personality disorder (BPD). While it's no secret that living with an individual afflicted with either of these psychological ailments can be quite difficult, the good news is that you've already begun the quest towards establishing a healthier relationship. Though it will involve work, patience, and some life alterations, individuals who are involved in relationships with narcissists or people with BPD can rediscover a rewarding relationship built on love and trust. We'll explain how throughout this guide.

To outsiders who don't understand the complexities of narcissism or BPD, it may seem easy or inconsequential to suggest a solution such as simply "walking away" from a relationship plagued by these issues. Yet, the fact of the matter is that narcissists and BPD sufferers need help, just like anyone else who's battling a mental or physical ailment. Even more promising is the fact that they, too, can regain or discover a healthy mental state in which their worries, behaviors, and anxieties can be alleviated so they (and their partners) no longer have to suffer.

If you've found yourself in a relationship that's marked by narcissism or BPD, there's a great sense of hope that you can turn things around and find a happy and healthy committed relationship. By following the tips listed in this guide, you can move towards a place of better understanding in which you'll no longer have to walk on eggshells to run the risk of upsetting your partner.

You've come to this guide in search for help, and that's what you'll find. Most likely, you've invested a great deal of time, emotion, and resources into your relationship and you aren't willing to simply throw it away. Despite what people may have told you, you don't have to. If your partner is willing to make improvements to work towards bettering your relationship, then there is great potential for you both to get to a place of blissful ease amongst one another.

Chapter 1:
Narcissism and BPD:
What are these Conditions?

The term "narcissist" tends to be thrown around without much regard for its actual psychological definition. Despite the fact that narcissism is typically associated with unfavorable characteristics and behaviors, many people fail to realize that it is, in fact, a personality disorder. In other words, narcissism is typically developed over a period of time, and it's actually a problem that creates suffering on multiple levels. Not only does it affect the people who are emotionally tied to the narcissist, but the sufferer may develop such a deep-rooted obsession with him or herself that eventually, he or she becomes entirely isolated from loved ones.

Narcissism isn't simply the act of exuding an air of extreme arrogance; it goes much deeper than that on a psychological level. Narcissists seek constant praise and fulfillment to reassure their own accomplishments and positive qualities. They seek out individuals who can feed them with attention and praise, and they may even exploit others for their own personal gain. Most often, narcissists are unable to establish a sense of empathy towards other individuals.

It's important to keep in mind that a person may have narcissistic traits without actually having narcissistic personality disorder. Someone may come across as arrogant, overly confident, or entirely self-centered, but that doesn't necessarily mean that he or she would be clinically diagnosed with narcissistic personality disorder. In order to have this mental illness, one must have an entirely exaggerated perspective about him or herself.

Another facet of narcissism that's commonly overlooked is that it can actually be healthy, to a degree. In fact, everyone is narcissistic to some point: we all take care of ourselves on a regular basis, which means that to an extent, we do care about our own well-being and how we are perceived by others. Unhealthy narcissism, or narcissistic personality disorder, takes these concepts to extreme levels. When someone is a narcissist, it means that he or she is wholly absorbed in his or her own existence.

This, of course, is quite a disadvantage for those involved in a narcissist's life. Not only does it become difficult to appease an individual who is constantly striving for admiration and reassurance, but it can be emotionally taxing to have to meet the overwhelming demands that a narcissist typically sets forth. Also, this may come across as an extremely troubling fact to grasp, but the truth is that narcissists rarely are able to see other individuals as emotional beings with real needs - in most cases, the narcissist is instead focused on how others can be used to his or her advantage. In other words, you are likely in the narcissist's life because you are a functional being that serves a specific purpose which acts to his or her advantage.

Like many afflictions of the mind, though, narcissism typically points to a specific troubling issue or series of events that took place throughout a person's upbringing. Oftentimes, narcissists develop false personas after undergoing a major trauma at some point during their early lives. Because the issue they're faced with is so difficult and complex for a young individual to handle, they develop a barrier to shield themselves from the outside world, thereby restricting their ability to develop psychologically in the same way that most people do.

This does not mean, however, that narcissists are incapable of handling their emotions in a healthy manner. They are fully capable of healing, and while it may be difficult, they can overcome emotional hurdles which will allow them to communicate openly and honestly with their partners.

Individuals with BPD are different from narcissists in the fact that they tend to make impulsive decisions, and their behavior can become unstable or even self-harming. People with BPD typically come across as being irritable or easily angered.

If you're involved in a relationship with an individual who has BPD, it can be difficult for you to know what to expect from him or her. At times, a BPD individual will idealize others, while at the other extreme, they can become devaluing and degrading. Thus, you might feel valuable and appreciated by your partner in one moment, only to feel as though you've disappointed them in the next. The roller-coaster experience can take a great toll on anyone living with a person who has BPD.

Most often, BPD presents itself by early adulthood, though the illness might have started as young as childhood. Like narcissism, the cause of BPD can't be blamed on the person who suffers from it - it, too, can be caused by antagonistic childhood experiences. BPD has also been linked to genetics, and there's a possibility that it could also stem from an issue within a specific area of the brain that regulates stress and emotions.

At its core, BPD prevents a person from being able to manage his or her emotions properly. Yet, the confusing part of BPD is the fact that it won't always affect all of the relationships that the individual is involved in - sometimes, in fact, it might only affect one relationship. It's important not to take this personally - it's simply an aspect of the disease that varies from person to person.

BPD can be misdiagnosed as bipolar disorder, so it's important to understand the difference between the two. BPD, like narcissism, often leads a person to greatly fear abandonment, even if this worry is wholly unjustified. Also, the impulsivity that often accompanies BDP can become self-damaging - eating disorders and substance abuse are common behaviors found in individuals who suffer from BPD.

Like narcissism, it's possible that someone can display certain characteristics that would be associated with BPD, yet not be diagnosed with the disorder. While it's considered to be somewhat of a "young" disease since it's only been recognized by the psychiatric community since the 1980s, it's possible that up to 14 million Americans are living with the illness, or roughly 5.9% of the population. Narcissism is potentially even more prevalent, and could affect up to 6.2%% of the population.

Chapter 2:
How Can You Tell a Narcissist When Courting?

You cannot blame someone for an ailment, can you? But at the same time, you want to know what you are getting yourself into before you commit to someone, presumably, for life. That is why it will suit you to be aware when the person you are dating has a mental disorder like narcissism. It would not be good for your relationship if you tied the knot with a narcissistic partner only to identify the condition for what it is later on and realizing you bit more than you could chew. Yet you may know the reality in advance and decide to remain in the relationship and help the person through the healing process.

Here are some narcissistic tendencies that exclaim – red flag!

Extended chase

Do you expect a show of affection from your partner during the courting period? Rhetorical, isn't it? And do you expect to show affection yourself? That one too... In fact, this is not something either of you plans. It just happens. Call it something out of attraction, chemistry... well – the show of affection goes both ways.

However, once you are both comfortable with where you stand in each other's life, you cease to give too much weight to the show of affection as there are other aspects of your relationship that speak volumes about the seriousness of your relationship. This is now the part where narcissistic partners do not seem to get it. They will express to you, either in behavior or words, that they take it you are not serious with the relationship because you have not done something to show affection; or you have not complimented them – mark you, not EVER – but recently. A narcissistic partner demands an incessant flow of compliments and other tangible deeds that indicate 'affection'. It is like affirmation, reaffirmation, and yet more affirmation. And after sometime you begin wondering, are they in, are they out, or are they uncertain? What you may not know is that even when they declare they are in for keeps, the demand for affection does not cease.

Listen to them but don't expect an audience

That's the narcissist – demanding your full attention when they speak, whether they are telling you about their day's exciting experiences or whether they are ventilating about something they did not like. On the contrast, you will be disappointed if you expect them to pay attention to you when you are talking about yourself and your experiences; least of all your problems. Well, life is about them. So if you are speaking about yourself, you need to show clearly how that bit relates specifically and primarily to your narcissistic partner and his/her welfare. Soon you will get it loud and clear – that is, if you do not choose to bury your head in the sand – your problems are singularly yours and not worth their time; and that their problems are central to the relationship and it is upon your both to solve them.

Do not plan unless they give a nod

Your narcissistic partner subjects every decision you make to scrutiny with a view to seeing if they are going to benefit socially, financially, however – just being in the middle of things is their struggle. Sometimes they would rather you watched the Big Game alone in the sitting room. Can you go out and join your friends? No! Can you invite your friends over? Oh, no! So, just sit indoors and watch the game? Yes – with a thousand and one distractions, because anyway, your narcissistic partner is not interested football let alone the Super Bowl!

In short, they make their decisions independently, but any decision you make depends on them.

Give them full attention all the time

Does your narcissistic partner expect to get your full attention at the expense of everyone else? Yes, that's it! It does not matter who the others are – parents, siblings, friends... The world a narcissist lives in has them as the nucleus irrespective of how long you have known them and how long you have known the other people. The narcissist takes this position as so natural that they see no shame in letting other people know it. In fact, the happiest day for a narcissist is when you shower them with compliments all day long. In fact, it seems unlikely they appreciate the meaning of the word 'flattery'.

They shield you from others

Being shielded could be a good thing – right? Well, not if you are being shielded from people you care about. What good is protection if it is centered on people you have built healthy relationships with over the years? What good is it to you also if you cannot build new relationships? That seems like cutting off your past and building no future... Bluntly speaking, it looks like your narcissistic partner wants a world where you belong only with him/her alone. And in the meantime he/she is in a world where you are part of as well as other people.

Dare not voice criticism

The language and tone are immaterial but if you express anything that is tantamount to a minus, a deficiency or 'could do better' kind of attitude, brace yourself for a tantrum if not a fully erupted volcano. Narcissists easily freak out by the thought that anyone could fault them. Remember – everything about them is presumably excellent and anything that does not evolve around them is faulty.

Your partner comes before you 360°

That means under no circumstances does your narcissistic partner put you or your needs before theirs. Try talking to them about prioritizing anything concerning you and you see them behave like you are trying to turn the world inside out. Like you are suggesting the stars drop down and carpet the grounds while sand from the ground flies up and covers the skies – unimaginable!

The ball is now in your court. Just remember that narcissism is a mental disorder. Sometimes it goes by the reference Narcissistic Personality Disorder (NPD) and its flagship behaviors are self conceit; selfishness; and a misplaced sense of self importance.

Chapter 3:
How to Identify Narcissists at Your Workplace

How do narcissists survive at the workplace considering they are self centered individuals? That is something you may, understandably, wonder, especially considering there are the organization's goals to think about. Well, you can identify narcissists at the workplace by their bullying tendencies. And bullying is not their only red flag. Narcissists are arrogant too.

And if you think it is difficult to get a narcissist partner to seek medical treatment, double that difficulty when it comes to a narcissist at the workplace. First of all they belong to that category of employees with an inflated ego. How dare you talk of the possibility of a medical problem with them, let alone a mental one? And with the natural tendencies of a narcissist, most people get exhausted dealing with them and so they just let them have their way. Therefore, narcissists are used to having their way at work. Besides, they see no reason to change their behavior since, in their way of thinking, their way is always right. In any case, if ever and whenever anything goes wrong, it is, by default, the fault of the next fellow – the narcissist can do no wrong in his/her view.

What else screams, narcissist, at work?

They are great manipulators

Among the people bosses like is the narcissist. And you should not imagine it is because bosses like egoistic individuals – no. It is just that narcissists have a charming way of getting close to those who matter. Even if it means doing some funny stuff to control the boss' mind they'll do it. And in most workplaces, if the boss is on your side, who can be against you? (*Biblical paraphrasing...*)

They lie without batting an eyelid

There are many times that narcissists get hired on the basis of their lies. And once on the inside, many times they get promoted or get into positions of advantage on the basis of lies.

A narcissistic boss ruthlessly pursues success

The reason a narcissistic boss goes all out for success is not the normal one of having the organization's advantage at heart – hardly. The main reason is personal; to shine as an individual against the performance of other people within the organization. And to that end, they are ruthless when dealing with people under them.

A narcissist boss does not take criticism

Not only does a narcissistic boss fail to take criticism kindly, they often punish it. So people around such a leader get used to not pointing out any weak areas.

A narcissist boss takes credit solely

This happens even when the good ideas came from other employees at the workplace. A narcissist cannot bring himself/herself to give credit to other people even when it is due because to them the limelight should always be on them.

A narcissistic boss is very controlling

If you are thinking of a boss who lets people exercise their critical thinking and implement policies the best way they know how, you will not find that if your boss is narcissistic. Narcissist bosses demand that you do things their way. Even in situations where the culture encourages free thinking, anyone whose immediate supervisor or manager is a narcissist suffers manipulation so that you hardly really enjoy that freedom. A narcissistic boss manipulates you so that at the end of the day you end up doing his/her bidding.

It is normal for them to throw tantrums

Anytime a narcissistic boss feels like you are questioning their authority or even their methods; or any time they feel like they are losing full control of you, they throw tantrums. Often they go to extremes and recommend firing of employees on flimsy grounds. Remember whatever goes wrong around a narcissist is always someone else' fault irrespective of whether that person was following orders from the same senior – sounds twisted, but that is it.

Narcissistic bosses are abusive

If abuse is what will instill the fear of the boss into you so that you do their bidding, it is what the narcissist does. Many people have even come to accept abusive behavior from their bosses as normal, erroneously giving it names like strict, no-nonsense or something close to that. Yet in reality, a boss can be strict and still be open to criticism. He or she can be no-nonsense without being abusive.

Generally when you find it necessary to massage your boss' ego, chances are that you have a narcissist for a boss. And again your immediate instinct is not to put your raw ideas forth for consideration; instead you find yourself always weighing if there is a chance your ideas might antagonize your boss. So your life at the workplace becomes one of conflict avoidance, and getting used to someone else taking credit for your good work.

If you want to delve deep into the behavior of a narcissistic employee, there are two references that can help you - *(NPI, Raskin & Hall, 1981 and (Emmons, 1984)*. You will establish how special a narcissistic employee considers himself or herself; how much they lack in empathy; what a sense of entitlement they have; how much they hunger for admiration; their unsettling arrogance and haughtiness; and their excessive exploiting tendencies.

And what are the most telling signs of a narcissistic ordinary employee?

- Well, agreeable is one adjective you can give them particularly when you are new to them. They want to be in good books with you – remember? And that is for the sole reason of checking out the best way to manipulate you for their personal gain.

- Once you get to know them better, you are likely to begin questioning their emotional stability and conscientiousness.

- Narcissists have the tendency to dismiss others and their ideas. They are also abrasive.

- Owing to the combination of characteristics displayed by narcissists when relating to other people, there is hardly a favourable atmosphere for teamwork. Instead, narcissists bring in negative vibe and discord within a team.

- Narcissist employees bring in competitiveness that is negative; one that pitches them against other employees in a manner that makes the working environment unhealthy. The main negative aspect here is the way narcissists carry themselves with a sense of self importance and one that derides other people.

- Narcissists have a way of sowing distrust amongst people who have close associations.

- Narcissists are not dependable in giving self assessment. And mark you there are normally no prizes in situations of self assessment! Narcissists are known to exaggerate their level of capability and inflate their rating.

- Whenever it is made clear that someone else is a better performer than the narcissist, do not get surprised to hear disparaging remarks from the narcissist against the better performer.

- In any evaluation where the narcissist is not given the lead position, there is the likelihood of the narcissist to disparage the assessors themselves. Sometimes the narcissist can even manifest aggressive behaviour towards the person conducting the evaluation.

- Narcissists overrate themselves in a way that can put the group they belong to in jeopardy. They can, for instance, describe themselves as being adept at negotiation whereas it is just a display of overconfidence. If a business deal is at stake and the company lets a narcissist employee be the negotiator, the company risks losing the deal.

Chapter 4:
Narcissism from a Religious Perspective

Do you probably hold the notion that religious figures are free from selfish behavior? Well, that ideally might be the case, but really, when it comes to narcissism, it is a mental disorder; a health issue. And, of course, nobody, irrespective of their social standing, economic status or even religious inclination, is immune to health problems.

The complication sets in when the person who is meant to lead others out of exploitation and manipulation is the one carrying the mass of the problem. It becomes like a case of a blind person trying to lead the way for everyone else. Would you expect any less than confusion, stumbling and inter-personal friction?

Incidentally, you cannot use nature as an excuse for narcissism as much it is tempting to cover for religious leaders. They, too, acquire narcissism as they grow up. Remember that just like everyone else, religious leaders are part of this society that is ridden with hedonistic tendencies. If such a consumer driven society produces narcissists in big numbers, how would anyone be surprised that some leaders are narcissistic, whatever their occupation?

A Resurrection Church bishop from Brooklyn in New York, Joseph Mattera, takes us through some traits that can tell you when a religious leader is narcissistic. Here they are:

Seeking to be served instead of serving

Ever heard of servant leadership? That is what everyone expects of religious leaders. And quoting the Bible, the gospel of Matthew, chapter 20:26 – 28, Bishop Mattera says Jesus, the Biblical son of God, advocated for leaders to serve their followers and not vice-versa and he did lead by example.

So when you see a religious leader promoting people within a religious institution based on how well they sing his or her praises and how fast those people are to do the leader's bidding; and in the process the leader is relegating competence and merit to the back banner, you need to realize you have a narcissistic leader right there. Of course, you should not misconstrue loyalty to mean narcissism – there is no evil in expecting loyalty. Expecting loyalty can only become evil and an element of narcissism if it is self-serving to the leader and demeaning to the person showing loyalty.

Desiring the perks without readiness to bear the pain

Ever heard of *no pain, no gain*? And maybe you have heard too about the purest gold having had to pass through fire. In fact, the Holy Bible talks about this position in both the Old Testament (try Job) and the New Testament (in 1 Peter). There is no way you are going to have it all rosy without cutting a sweat or losing an iota of sleep. You would not be living on earth – possibly some utopia. After all, don't the beautiful roses themselves have pricking thorns? The only person who expects praise and honor; recognition and compliments; all without having to tire or make some sacrifice is the narcissist.

The funny part is that you will rarely find this narcissistic behavior with your CEO. In religious circles, you will rarely identify it with the pope, your Imam, or the rest of the religious leaders at the very top. In fact, the topmost heads of institutions appreciate that there is a rough and tough side to their prestigious positions. And so, when they acknowledge your appreciation, it is usually with sincere humility; and the appreciation you give, the title they hold, the prestige that comes with the position, are well deserved. The ruffling comes when you get to the secondary leaders.

Some want to get as much recognition and attention as the top leader. The unsettling bit about this is that they are not willing to do what it takes to deserve the top position. Are they ready to take the blame when things go wrong in the institution? Forget it! They may possibly even be among the lot eagerly pointing at where the buck stops – the topmost, of course. According to Bishop Mattera, the narcissistic religious leader wants to enjoy the perks that come with leadership in the ministry but does not want to bear the pain that comes with the ministry.

Elevating personal needs before those of the masses

Is your religious leader focused significantly on his or her personal comfort at the expense of your comfort as followers? Do you notice any obsession with his or her personal wellbeing? Is your leader too much dedicated to personal financial success and prestige? If you notice all that with your leader without noticing anything noteworthy to promote the welfare of the masses, you are looking at a narcissist. And there is even the danger of a narcissist leader fleecing the institution to the bone.

If you look at the gospel of John, chapter 10, in the Holy Bible, you will notice that a genuine spiritual leader is expected to lay his life for the sheep he leads – not to use the sheep for self aggrandizement. And in Islam you will find examples where leaders have made sacrifices for the common good. In fact, in Islam they teach how Isa, the Prophet, suffered and bore taunts from the Jews for the sake of achieving a 'holy aim'. As for the Hindu, you will not have to go far. You have Mahatma

Gandhi who showed the modern world what servant leadership is all about.

Propensity to accumulate material wealth

Religious leaders who are narcissistic are self indulgent as far as material wealth goes. You may even notice their desire to possess prestigious items and a tendency to engage in earthly pleasures including dining in exclusive restaurants; excessive visits to entertainment spots; and so on. They are often in the front line in the chase for the most recent car model; the newest Smartphone; laptop and so on; and they may also go for designer clothes on the institution's budget. Suffice it to say, these narcissistic leaders are high on spending and satisfying their personal desires and low on service delivery to the people.

Desiring to be adored

Are you frank when speaking to your leader the same way you are with your equals? Well, you cannot then be in good books with the narcissist in religious leadership. They want sycophants around them – people who will never tell them when they are over-indulging or when they are neglecting the flock. They actually love people who keep telling them how great and impressive they are even if it is in relation to all the vain things the leaders have accumulated at the expense of the ministry. Flattery is a delicacy they consume with much relish.

They use and discard people

Narcissist religious leaders can treat you like the most valued person the earth has ever seen as long as they are courting you to help accomplish a selfish need. However, no sooner do you serve their purpose than they drop you like a hot piece of iron rod. To such leaders, other people are at their disposal to use for their own success and satisfaction. In short, to a narcissist, you are no different from the objects used to facilitate a process. Spiritual as they may claim to be, narcissist leaders fail to treat other people as creatures of equal importance even when that is a fundamental principle across most religions, if not all.

Having no interest in other people's problems

Do narcissistic religious leaders seek audience when they have problems in their career or other spheres of life? Of course, they do. Do they get it? Obviously, religious leaders are respected within the institution and beyond and so it is easy for them to get audience when they need it. In any case, it is normal human nature to listen when others have problems to share so that you can at least empathize, if not practically contribute to the solution.

Big question – does the narcissistic religious leader pay attention when you have problems to share? No – simple and clear! To the narcissist, any conversation worth participating in is that which revolves around their interest or concern. If you are in a group and a general problem is being discussed, you are likely to notice that the narcissist is emotionally closed. Problems whose solutions are not going to benefit the narcissist directly are a sheer waste of time as far as the narcissist is concerned.

Not appreciating other people's ideas

The question that comes to the narcissist's mind whenever someone makes a suggestion is, eh…what's in it for me? How will I benefit from this idea? And if there is no pointer towards some personal benefit, you can take your idea to the open market because the narcissist has no intention of supporting it. Objectivity is not the narcissist's forte, notwithstanding the fact that the narcissist is religious; and not just religious, but in a position of leadership.

Something else – just as narcissists reject your idea, they also have no intention of modifying or dropping an idea that they have. You need to keep in mind that narcissists are always right as far as they are concerned. And they make no wrong choices; if a narcissist's choice ends up being wrong, it is always someone else's fault. Oh, sorry – there is an exception to this behavior of clinging to an own idea. The minute the narcissist identifies another idea that is bound to benefit him or her better, the earlier one can now go – actually MUST go. The best to a narcissist is the one with the most gain; and not spiritually for that matter.

Narcissists barely, if at all, succeed in intimate emotional relationships

Is it surprising that relationships with a narcissist fail to last long? It actually shouldn't be. Narcissists do not care about the needs of anyone else irrespective of their relationship. Whenever they seem to care, it is because they are tuning you to reward them in an even greater way. They are all about manipulation and self fulfillment. And if you think you are tight with a narcissist, you will realize whom you are dealing with when the fun you provide runs out; and the entertainment you provide and gossip is no longer as interesting. Then the narcissist begins to lose interest in you.

Narcissists hardly survive in relationships whenever there is need for personal sacrifice. How can they bring themselves to sacrifice time, attention and resources for the sake of others when, deep ingrained in them is the belief that their position is similar to that of the sun where the planets revolve around it? That is why, even for a spiritual leader, a happy marriage, when the leader is narcissistic, hardly goes beyond the honeymoon period when the narcissist is getting full attention and everything is rosy and fun.

But when it comes to sharing the spouse' attention with the children, it ruins the narcissist's life. Instead of having to share attention, finances and other resources with the couple's own children, with all the theology in the head and religious books in the office, the narcissist partner prefers to escape to another relationship; to hobbies; to long entertainment periods; and so on. Only divine intervention can save such a relationship.

Being prone to adulterous behavior

Unfortunate as it is in the realm of spiritual leadership, many are the times that narcissistic religious leaders fall for flattery from the opposite sex and end up in adulterous relationships. When it is clear that what you long for is praise irrespective of how genuine or not it is, there are many people willing to provide it. Incidentally, such providers also gauge what there is in it for them.

It is important to note that narcissistic religious leaders, just like other narcissists, are not emotionally attached to anyone; not even those that appear close to them. Theirs is physical attachment where the pleasure they can derive from the relationship is all that matters. It is usual, therefore, to find narcissistic religious leaders being addicted to pornography. Just as in the case of material wealth, they will do about anything to satisfy themselves physically as long as it does not call for emotional attachment.

Chapter 5:
Where to Begin

Before you can act on improving your loved one's condition, it's important to first make sure that he or she truly does have either of these disorders. Typically, individuals who are living with narcissistic personality disorder or BPD aren't aware of the fact that they have it, and it's quite rare for them to seek out psychiatric help on their own.

Remember, displaying certain behaviors that might resemble narcissistic personality disorder or BPD doesn't necessarily mean that your loved one is afflicted with either of these mental illnesses. Yet, he or she may still need psychiatric help. For example, if your significant other seems to have an obsession with attaining success and power, it could just be that he or she may be experiencing some self-confidence issues and would still benefit from therapy sessions. If he or she seeks constant attention and praise *and* seems to lack the ability to empathize with others, there's a good chance that your loved one will be diagnosed with narcissistic personality disorder. Likewise, if your loved one is harming him or herself in a certain way, it doesn't mean that he or she definitely has BPD; but it's still important to seek psychological help so as to combat the issue.

Most importantly, your loved one is going to require a proper diagnosis. We live in a world in which information is at our fingertips; thus, it can become quite easy to make an improper self-diagnosis. Truly, when it comes to our mental and physical wellbeing, it's always important to seek professional help. This is no different - although this guide will help steer you in the proper direction and help you to handle the difficulties associated with these illnesses, your loved one will still need to visit a mental health professional who can provide a proper diagnosis. While general practitioners typically aren't trained in these specific realms, your family doctor may be able to recommend a psychologist or psychiatrist who specializes in these areas.

One thing that many people wonder about - yet are too unsure to ask - is what kind of tests need to be performed to detect narcissistic personality disorder or BPD. You'll probably be glad to know that there aren't any genetic, blood, or lab tests that need to be conducted in order to make this diagnosis. Mental health professionals can detect personality disorders simply by meeting with your loved one and evaluating symptoms and his or her history.

It's common for individuals who are involved in a relationship with a person who's suffering from a mental illness to feel lost and helpless. Most likely, you've already experienced these types of feelings; of course, you *want* to help, but perhaps you're unsure of where to start. You may even be a bit fearful of how your loved one will react. After all, you may have already had to alter your behavior to some extent, so as to avoid exacerbating the compounding issues that result from your loved one's disease. You don't intend to upset him or her even more or make the struggle even more difficult.

Your job isn't going to be easy, but taking the first step is going to be the most difficult part. After that, everything will be done in order to move towards improvement. So, before you begin, remember to keep in mind that whatever happens throughout the journey, you must not take your loved one's behaviors personally. He or she may act out or show anger towards you, but it doesn't mean that you've done anything wrong. In fact, showing love and support and learning as much about his or her illness (which is what you're doing by reading this guide) are the only things that you can do to help.

When you first approach your loved one to let him or her know that you're concerned, you may be met with resistance. That's why one of the most crucial aspects you'll need to keep in mind moving forward is that you'll have to move slowly. The journey towards achieving a healthier mental state is an arduous one, so patience plays a huge role in avoiding further issues. You'll need to approach it so that you are making your loved one fully aware of the fact that you're coming from a place of love and support. Even if you feel emotionally exhausted or frustrated, you have to let your loved one know that you care about him or her.

You might want to approach it simply by expressing your honest concern and asking your loved one if he or she needs help with anything, whether there's anything that he or she wants to talk about, or even telling him or her frankly that you've been worried lately. Remember to be delicate, yet honest. Even if you feel as though you've had to curb your behavior in any way or walk on eggshells to appease your loved one in the past, you're aiming for positive change here, so now is the time to be direct and straightforward. If you're going to initiate any kind of change, you can't skirt around the issue.

Oftentimes, individuals suffering from mental illness will deny the problem. This can occur due to a wide variety of reasons, but many people feel a deep sense of embarrassment or even disbelief when it comes to a mental illness diagnosis. In this situation, it may benefit you to equate mental illness to physical illness: remind your loved one that it can happen to anyone and that it's nothing to be ashamed about. State that while it's unfortunate that he or she is suffering, the only way to heal is to get help.

Again, keep in mind that it may take some time for your loved one to come around to this idea. Initial progress can be especially slow-moving for mental health sufferers, but that doesn't mean that it's impossible. Even if you need to revisit the issue a couple of times before your loved one expresses any kind of willingness to act on it, there's always hope. Although it may seem extreme, you might also want to consider the option of staging an intervention simply to get your loved one to the point at which he or she recognizes a need for help. Remember, though, that everyone is different. What works for some people might not work for others. Also keep in mind that you may be met with anger, resentment, or other forms of negativity from your loved one at first. These are common reactions and must not be taken personally.

Chapter 6:
How Narcissism Varies From BPD

Any dispute you could do well without the two conditions? Of course, not! Both Narcissism and BPD are mental conditions which, when they afflict someone close to you, normalcy becomes a rarity in your life. They are conditions that put you on edge and often walking on eggshells – some kind of social prison where you cannot express yourself spontaneously for fear of invoking eruptive emotions from the other person. And at any one time you can never predict what those people are going to come up with because they are known to translate situations in negative ways, even when everyone else sees those same situations as just plain and normal. On casual evaluation, therefore, it may not be easy to tell if your person has BPD or NPD.

In fact, as per the *Diagnostic and Statistical Manual of Mental Disorders* (DSM-IV), both BPD and NPD make a person exhibit behavior that is erratic; emotional; and also dramatic. And one significant factor that sits well with both of them is antagonism – that is like the trademark of both. Antagonizing people around them is what those with BPD and NPD are best at. And both BPD and NPD have co-morbidity with other mental conditions at a rate of 25% to 37%. Pretty high, that rate! No wonder BPD and NPD are such complex conditions to deal with.

Before delving into the co-morbidity of each of the two mental disorders, let us simplify what they share here below:

- None of them cares about anyone else' feelings but theirs

- Both categories see the world as revolving around them

- They fear abandonment and get anxious at the thought

- They both demand constant attention

- They have poor relationships with family and colleagues at work; and are equally poor at building healthy social relationships.

- Their behavior is usually erratic; unduly emotional; and they often exhibit behavior that is self dramatizing.

And as has already been mentioned, people with either personality disorder have anger issues; misplaced sense of self; and the tendency to have fluctuating views about someone – one time idealizing them and the next devaluing the same individuals.

What other conditions accompany BPD, for example?

Actually, there are a number of other conditions prevalent whenever someone has Borderline Personality Disorder. Do not get surprised to see such a person suffering depression to some extent or even having bipolar disorder. In such circumstances, what you often notice is pronounced mood swings. And often you may realize they have anxiety disorders. Sometimes such people also get trapped in substance abuse. Other times they suffer Post Traumatic Stress Disorder (PTSD). Also among people with BPD are those that have bulimia or other eating disorders. A good number also suffers attention deficiency hyperactivity disorder. So sometimes when you are talking of a partner with BPD, you are actually looking at someone presenting a significantly heavy package to deal with.

And what other conditions accompany NPD?

Narcissists also bring with them a difficult package to deal with. For some that package contains *Dysthmia*, or what you can simply describe as Persistent Depressive Disorder. Then there is *anorexia nervosa* and other feeding disorders. Narcissists also tend to engage in addictive tendencies including substance abuse. A significant number of them even use cocaine. And some suffer Paranoid Personality Disorder.

However, the reality is that each one of these disorders – BPD and NPD – is distinct and needs to be handled differently when it comes to therapy. How you get to normalize life when living with a person with BPD and one with NPD also calls for varied approaches.

This Is How Borderline Personality Disorder Manifests Most Times

First of all you need to accept that mood swings are part of the package. And these can last from short spells of a couple of minutes to long periods of even hours. And we could mention here that prevalence of BPD is higher in women than in men – in fact, three times higher in women. The impulsive behavior that can be associated with BPD begins to show in early adulthood. Here is how to identify it:

They make frantic endeavors to avoid abandonment

People with BPD make these frantic endeavors even when there is no threat of abandonment in reality. What this implies is that people with BPD live in constant fear of being abandoned.

They suffer what, in psychology, they call splitting behavior

There are times people with BPD are unrecognizable when relating to you owing to their changing behavior. It may shock you that the same person who only recently was singing your praises is now demonizing you in all possible terms. You are dealing with people of extremes; people whose thinking does not accommodate middle ground. First of all, if you do not fall for their suggestion in totality, you become the devil incarnate; but when you embrace what they want, you become the angel who can do no evil. The basis is usually simple – are you fulfilling their needs now or are you frustrating them?

They suffer from identity disturbance

When a person suffers identity disturbance, they carry an image of themselves that is distorted. They may have low self esteem or even be pessimistic in a way that is clearly illogical. There are times too that they have contradictory feelings about themselves – sometimes positive and other times negative. Sometimes they portray healthy thinking and other times negative. Likewise you may find them full of life one day and the next they just appear lethargic. Suffice it to say when it comes to people with BPD, their sense of self is unstable.

They are impulsive even where discipline is paramount

For most of them, people with BPD act on impulse in a way that is self damaging when it comes to some behavior requiring self control. A person with BPD is known for at least two among the excesses of binge eating; overspending; reckless sex; substance abuse; careless driving; among others.

Suicidal behavior that is recurrent

Such suicidal behavior has signs in form of threats; gestures; and sometimes mutilating oneself.

Affective instability

This refers to the rapid and repeated abrupt mood shifts that a person with BPD experiences. In the midst of this is intense *dysphoria*, where the person feels extremely dissatisfied with life. And these people are also irritable during these episodes. Often they have their anxiety levels rising to discomforting levels, lasting hours – and on occasion, a few days.

Emptiness

People with BPD chronically experience a sense of emptiness.

Uncontrolled and misplaced anger

Often people with BPD get intensely angry in a way that other people cannot comprehend. They are constantly angry; losing temper at will; and sometimes they even engage in physical fights.

They suffer paranoid ideation

Getting constantly suspicious of other people's intentions towards you is what paranoid ideation is about. Sometimes you even believe that other people are on a mission to persecute you or harass you.

And this Is How Narcissism Manifests Most Times

We have already alluded to that feeling of superiority that a narcissist has – that exaggerated sense of self importance. Yet this same person feels insecure and has self esteem that is very fragile. Those are some of the contradictions that complicate life with a narcissist. You hardly know what personality trait is going to prevail in any one day. But the hallmark, as you may have deduced by now, is the sheer absence of empathy as relates to other people.

Contrary to the case of BPD, narcissism is more prevalent in men than in women. And this behavior may draw your attention when you observe arrogance; dominance; behavior that tends to say, here is someone superior; a hard push for power; and as usual, glaring lack of empathy. When it comes to intimate relationships, the partner with NPD usually chooses to bolt out when it strikes them that their partner is likely to leave them.

From early adulthood, you may begin to observe in a person with NPD behavior of grandiosity whose pattern is evidently pervasive; and sometimes it is just in fantasy. You may also notice the person's intense desire to be admired. Missing empathy is, of course, something you cannot miss to notice with a narcissist.

Here is how to identify a case of NPD

- You find them narrating their exemplary achievements and outstanding talents but there is really nothing to show for it. And yet they expect you to take their word for it and consequently treat them as superior. You could look at this behavior as an exaggerated sense of self importance.

- A person with NPD is pre-occupied with imagination of limitless power; outstanding brilliance; striking beauty; or even ideal love.

- You may notice that they have misplaced beliefs – like the belief that they are special and also unique; believing that for that matter only special people can understand them. In fact, owing to that misplaced belief, a narcissist believes in relating only with special people and people of high status.

- A narcissist demands excessive admiration.

- A narcissist always expects special treatment. That is the sense of entitlement mentioned earlier on in the book.

- A narcissist has exploitative tendencies; always taking advantage of other people to achieve what he or she wants.

- Narcissists cannot empathize with other people. They are not affected by the needs or feelings of other people.

- They are of a jealous nature and they also believe that other people are jealous of them.

- They carry themselves with haughtiness and arrogance.

Chapter 7:
Strategies for Living with a Narcissist

If you're determined to stay with your loved one even after you've established the fact that he or she is living with narcissistic personality disorder, then there are ways in which you can behave and think so as to create a healthier, less stressful relationship. Hopefully, you've approached your loved one and encouraged him or her to seek help from a mental health professional. While therapy sessions may promote healthier behaviors and ultimately move your relationship toward a happier place, your loved one may still hang on to certain behaviors or facets of his or her personality that can be difficult to deal with. Or, these behaviors may diminish greatly over time. Either way, you can practice the following skills in the meantime to ease tension and preserve your own mental wellbeing.

For one thing, you must learn to identify non-negotiable aspects of your life from those that can be compromised. In other words, living with narcissists means that you'll have to choose your battles. You'll find that you can't allow every little thing to upset you, and even if something does upset you slightly, it might not even be worth fighting over. Yet, on the other hand, there are certain things that simply cannot be tolerated or negotiated. For instance, if your loved one has frivolous spending habits that are pushing the two of you into serious debt, that's a behavior that ultimately must be stopped. Even if approaching the subject is stressful and difficult, you must find a common ground upon which you can agree. You don't have to have the exact same perspective on money, but reckless behavior can't be ignored. Figure out your own personal non-negotiable relationship matters, and remember to always hold firm when it comes to those. Also, while this should go without saying, one non-negotiable matter should be avoiding any behavior that will cause you physical harm. Regardless of how mentally ill a person may be, you should never subject yourself to domestic violence. Seek help immediately if that's the case.

Another thing you can do to cope with living with a narcissist is to learn how to trust your instincts. There may be times when your loved one tries to convince you that he or she never said something which you are certain he or she certainly did say. Or, perhaps your loved one will insist that something different was said. There may be times in which you think you're going crazy - don't. Rely on your instincts, and you'll fare better. Don't let the narcissist convince you of something when you're certain that something else entirely different took place. It's possible that your loved one is purposely acting out maliciously, or it could also be that he or she actually did forget what was said in the first place, but is just using this point in your conversation to work to his or her advantage in the present moment. Hopefully, if your loved one is working with a therapist, he or she will learn about the repercussions of this kind of behavior and will instead learn to rely on honestly. Until then, though, learn to trust your own judgment.

Likewise, it's important for you to be able to maintain honesty as well, not only in your romantic relationship, but in other relationships, as well. In other words, if you have another loved one, such as a relative or friend that you can trust and confide in, it may help you to share your experiences with him or her. An outside perspective can be extremely beneficial when it comes to living with someone who has a mental illness. It might also help to alleviate some of your frustration, because you can share your thoughts and experiences in an honest manner. Likewise, if you've been covering up your loved one's behaviors for a long period of time, you might find that it's actually easiest just to come forth and explain the situation to family members and friends. Remind them that you're seeking help and working to improve the situation.

When it comes to handling emotional outbursts, you may need to walk away from your loved one temporarily. Yet, make it known that this type of behavior is unacceptable. While it's true that everyone needs to let of steam from time to time, it shouldn't take place in a way that's malicious or wholly offensive to you. If you've been disrespected or degraded, you need to show your loved one that it was unfair and that you're hurt. Allow him or her to acknowledge the fact that you're disappointed, and ask for an apology. If your loved one won't oblige, tell him or her that you'll be willing to work things out once you are treated respectfully.

Your ability to foster your own sense of self-esteem will also be crucial. Narcissists are typically concerned only with their own needs; thus, yours will be overlooked frequently, if not altogether ignored. Remember that if you're feeling undervalued or underappreciated, it's not a signal that you're doing something wrong. Your loved one's mental illness has caused him or her to ignore your needs. Again, though, if you are both committed to making it work and seeking help, there's a good chance that your relationship will get easier, and in time, you'll begin to feel more valued.

Finally, since we discussed the importance of establishing which factors in your relationship are non-negotiable, you'll also have to develop strong negotiating skills. It may sound to you like you're coming up with skills for a job résumé, but in truth, developing these traits will make it much easier to cope with your loved one's narcissistic personality disorder. So, you'll need to learn how to refuse things. Your loved one may put up a very strong fight, but that shouldn't mean that he or she must automatically get his or her way. Become firm and resolute, and either develop a sense of confidence or rediscover the one that you've lost. There are many resources you can reference to better your negotiating skills. Don't feel guilty about reading up on them - you're not trying to "outsmart" your loved one; rather, you're learning real strategies for coping with his or her mental illness, at least until he or she can get to a better state of mental wellness.

Chapter 8:
How to End Manipulation by a Narcissist

Why the great concern about stopping manipulation by a narcissist? After all, people are always doing things to influence others. Whereas that is a valid question, it is important to note that the manipulation that a narcissist does is of an extreme degree. Narcissists are so engrossed in influencing things towards their end that they do not seem to realize it even when other people discover the manipulation for what it is. They do not even show any shame for their behavior, unlike someone caught trying to unduly influence a one-off deal.

Many people with narcissists who are close family relations or close friends often find themselves succumbing to their manipulation, not because they have not discovered this negative tendency, but because it seems much easier to give in than argue about it. Manipulation is part of a narcissist's behavior and so they do not find themselves expending unnecessary energy – to them, that's life. However, to other people, the antagonistic atmosphere created by a narcissist's attempt at manipulation can be draining. And the unfortunate bit is that the narcissist learns fast what buttons to press to get you unduly influenced. They capitalize on your fears and concerns or even your passions. Truth is, they can capitalize on any part of your personality to make things suit them.

A good number of adjectives have already been used to describe a narcissist, and others are still fitting. Within the context of trying to manipulate someone, the unappealing qualities that manifest themselves include being extremely emotional; defensive; reactive; hyper-sensitive; extremely demanding; and becoming furious at the remotest hint of criticism or even disapproval. Narcissists also project very many expectations and they are easily disappointed. The behavior of a narcissist partner or friend can make you edgy because they have this tendency of bringing up issues from the past from nowhere and making them appear like they have freshly occurred. And their pettiness can come in measures you never dreamt possible.

What is the natural reaction when the narcissistic behavior becomes overwhelming? Well, two contrasting reactions come to mind:

Falling into a rage

Does it help – you getting annoyed at your narcissist partner or colleague and probably getting into a verbal argument? As sure as the sun rises from the east, this does not help matters either for you or for your narcissistic partner.

Feeling sorry for the narcissist

Does this help? It surely doesn't. Narcissists just view that as opportunity for them to advance further their manipulation.

As has been pointed out already, narcissists know no empathy; at least not where giving is concerned. Yet they expect and enjoy receiving empathy. Now, whether you continue getting pissed off every time for the ridiculous behavior or you continue as the person perennially feeling sorry for the narcissist in your life, the outcome is hardly helpful. All you accomplish is establishing yourself as the feedlot for your narcissist so that whenever he or she feels the need for that surge of negative energy, you are game.

But then again, suppose you tried fighting fire with fire as alluded to earlier in this book? That might help. The point is, since you are dealing with someone who cannot afford empathy for anyone else; a person who feels that your concerns and issues should be yours to tackle singularly, why not work on reducing your concern too, the one you show almost on impulse, and leave your narcissist to handle his or her issues singularly too? Anyway, whatever step you decide to take, you need to be decisive. Lack of firmness can only lead you to a merry-go-round of pseudo-happiness and misery in life.

Improving Your Journey with a Narcissist

From what you have gathered so far, would it be surprising that anyone would seek skills to cope with the behavior of a narcissist? In fact, if you don't do that and you continue living with your narcissist partner or someone else with this disorder and who is close to you, you risk having a meltdown yourself. What's the use of accommodating the behavior of others to the extent that you go bonkers yourself?

Here are some tips to help you through your journey in life with a narcissist

You are not a loser if the narcissist chose to be with you

Oh yes! Narcissists do not go for losers. You are so successful they want you to illuminate their lives. With your brilliance and your charming nature, the narcissist wanted you as a trophy when they chose you – some piece of possession to show off with.

Turning you into ocean sludge

But open your eyes and see what the narcissist has been doing to you – tearing you down slowly by slowly, to establish that feeling of power and superiority. For the period you have spent with your narcissist, do you feel confident and attractive or even successful? Rarely, if at all... A narcissist could not have picked on a loser because then they would not have the satisfaction they so much hunger for. Losers do not provide anything high to bring down; nothing complex to dismantle; and nothing shiny to blur – and that is the twisted behavior of a narcissist.

You need to embark on regaining your confidence

Regaining what you have lost from your relationship with a narcissist can begin with regaining your self confidence. Much as a break from the narcissist would do you some good whilst the narcissist gets professional help, you may find yourself still living or associating with the person. It is important that you feel confident because it helps you deflect those toxic arrows that the narcissist inevitably continues to throw at you. With self confidence, you are able to:

- Keep your cool even when the narcissist tries to provoke you into an argument

- Recognize the narcissist's lies for what they are

Allow yourself to get the best

After a life of letting your narcissistic partner to enjoy the cream as you wait to consume the crumbs, it is time for you to allow yourself enjoyment because you deserve it. It is fine to sacrifice here and there for the common good, but that does not mean you let yourself be someone else's servant. And that is actually what a narcissist makes you. You need to reclaim your worth by demanding quality life as opposed to one of subservience. Demand to have your needs addressed first, for once – and that includes places you would like to visit; people you would like to associate with; and personal goals you would like to work on.

Practice walking away from temper driven tantrums

How horrible it is to encounter someone seething with rage! But then when it comes to narcissists, partner victims have said it is more intimidating to see a narcissist annoyed than any other look you could encounter. For one, enraged narcissists wear a face of disgust. Then their eyes are full of evil. That whole picture just makes your stomach churn. And how do you react to that? Well, ordinarily you pray you can quickly identify what it is the narcissist would have you do whether you enjoy doing it or not. You are fodder for their rage.

Sometimes your narcissist partner gets annoyed just because you corrected them; you disagreed with a certain point they made; or because of something that had nothing to do with you – like stumbling on a door frame. The message here is that it is time for you to stop trying to appease the narcissist in your life by making explanations or doing their bidding – simply walk away. If circumstances do not allow you to walk away, just rolling your eyes in a manner that says, what the heck, and totally ignoring them, might help. Here you are essentially avoiding a situation where you get to respond and hence give them courage to continue drawing your attention.

Avoid engaging in argument with a narcissist

Do you recall an earlier mention that the narcissist chose you because you had admirable qualities; with a mark of success?

So, definitely, he or she knows there is no way they can win an argument with you logically. Whenever they engage you in argument, expect incomprehensible stuff being dropped in a haphazard manner. And, of course, that is after you have repulsed an attempt at intimidation in a situation where the narcissists often throws you wild accusations; statements you can only term as crazy; and words made out of context.

And remember as a person who is mentally whole and stable, some behavior exhibited by the narcissist can be embarrassing to you in addition to draining your energy. Here is another instance where you just need to walk away instead of wasting your time with someone you pretty well know is not interested in listening and reasoning logically.

Work on re-establishing yourself

If you are true to yourself you will notice how much independence you have lost. Has your narcissist partner lost independence because of your relationship? Think hard and you will see that your narcissist partner gets to do what he or she wants at the end of the day. You need to begin doing something that you love as well, like a hobby, a class; something that makes you to feel free. You need to stop living like someone in a yoke.

Avoid falling into the trap of victim blaming

You won't be the first person to do this. Victim blaming is a tendency observed over the years. You begin telling people you know what you have been doing wrong when that is actually something to give you false psychological satisfaction that you have room to improve and bring your relationship with the narcissist back to normal. Well, that calculation can only be realized if the normal you are talking about is a repeat of the previous life – drama and more drama from your narcissist partner and you always giving way and doing your partner's bidding.

To get you back into their snare without them changing an ounce, you may find them also purporting to take part of the blame. But pay good attention; sooner or later that blame will be twisted to fall on your footstep. Since when did a narcissist take blame for anything? If you know that is not normal, can you not then see that your narcissist partner is simply manipulating you?

You need to stop taking their word seriously

Lying is the narcissist's middle name. You do not need to give a narcissist reason to lie – it is just part of them; kind of, engrained in their biological fabric. This may sound insane, but believe you me, a narcissist can tell you they have been sitting on Chair A when they have actually been sitting on Chair B, yet both of those chairs are replicas of each other and no location is better than the other.

And learn not to report anything a narcissist tells you to someone else without counter checking first otherwise you may end up making a fool of yourself and risk being labeled liar.

In case you decide you stick it out with the narcissist, just be realistic about whom you are living with – a liar who is prone to drama, deceit and conceit; and someone who is prone to antagonizing other people. Pretending you are living with a normal person and trying to cover for your narcissist partner would be one great mistake on your part. This is because you would only be making yourself vulnerable to the narcissist's toxic ways. Besides, you may end up becoming the subject of pity to observers who can see your vulnerabilities for what they are.

Chapter 9: Strategies for Living with someone who has BPD

BPD can fall anywhere on the spectrum, ranging from mild cases to severe. Living with the disease can make it difficult for individuals to maintain healthy relationships, jobs, and find a sense of continuity throughout life. At the same time, BPD sufferers can be extremely creative and inventive individuals. A BPD diagnosis doesn't diminish a person's worth by any means, and there are many misconceptions and stigmas that come with mental health illnesses. You know your loved one best of all, and chances are that you're willing to overcome this obstacle with him or her. If that's the case, then there are certain things you can do to make both of your lives easier.

For one thing, individuals who are involved in relationships with BPD sufferers are very likely to become recipients of misdirected anger. The level of anger could range from yelling or verbal maliciousness to downright rage. (As we mentioned previously, you should never stay in a relationship that requires you to withstand physical harm. Seek help immediately if you're a victim of domestic abuse.)

To avoid this rage, partners of BPD sufferers often find that they're forced to walk on eggshells. They want to avoid a blowout at all costs, so they internalize issues instead of expressing their thoughts and concerns in an honest manner. While this kind of behavior may help you get by in living with a person who has BPD, it certainly isn't healthy, and it's bound to take its toll on you over time.

Hopefully, if you've made the decision to stay in a relationship with the person who has BPD, you've both been able to come to the decision that he or she must seek help from a mental health expert to cultivate a healthier relationship and improve his or her own wellness. Like narcissistic individuals, though, people living with BPD may still exhibit some of their disease's typical behaviors during or following treatment. While you should maintain a level of patience and continue to offer support and understanding, there are also some specific strategies you can use to help you cope with your loved one's behaviors, which we'll discuss below.

For one thing, predictability is paramount for individuals living with BPD. Inconsistency can become frightening and confusing for them, even more so than it would for a person without BPD. Thus, you can ease the complications of your loved one's illness by always being consistent in your behaviors. In other words, if you tell your loved one that you're going to do something, make sure that you follow through. Avoid outbursts or blow ups, because that will only reinforce your loved one's borderline behavior. Also, it may be difficult for you to maintain a level attitude or a calm approach when you're faced with meltdowns or rage-filled outbreaks. Regardless of how you handle these issues, just make sure that you're consistent and respond the same way every time they occur. Don't feed into it, but also try not to respond with the same volatile behavior. *Don't fight fire w/ fire!*

It's also crucial that you don't fall into the role of becoming a codependent. What we mean by that is simply, you can't become your loved one's rescuer. It may be tempting to approach this issue as if you'll swoop in and save him or her, but the fact of the matter is that it's a battle he or she will need to attend to as well. You can't fix it for your loved one, but you can certainly be encouraging and supportive the whole way through. You will, however, need to encourage responsibility. If your loved one exhibits destructive behaviors stemming from his or her BPD, such as creating debt or abusing alcohol, you can't enable him or her to continue these acts. Allowing him or her to spend lots of money or continue drinking may appease your loved one temporarily, but it's unhealthy and it won't get you any closer to a solution. You need to be gentle but firm when you encourage responsibility.

Another thing you can do to maintain consistency throughout your relationship is to always be honest, no matter what the circumstances are. If you disagree with your loved one's assessment about a situation, you may not want to say it outright, so as to avoid a serious argument. For example, if your loved one loses his or her job and blames it on awful coworkers, yet you have a suspicion that his or her behavior may have played a role in the situation, you can simply offer honest feedback by saying, "I know it's a bad thing to lose your job." By doing this, you're letting your loved one know that you're coming from a place of understanding, and you're not berating him or her. Yet, you're not agreeing with your loved one outright, which could encourage future negative behaviors.

Another thing to remember when it comes to communicating with a person who has BPD is the fact that you'll need to bear in mind the importance of timing. There are good times and bad times to address particular issues. If a negative issue arises, it may be best to postpone the serious discussion that you'll need to have with your loved one. For example, if your loved one loses his or her job as a result of destructive behavior, you may want to postpone the discussion about the implications of the situation, or hold off on discussing anything relating to his or her BPD, for that matter. He or she will be extremely vulnerable directly following this type of situation, so it's important not to exacerbate the situation with a serious discussion.

When it comes to logics and emotions, people living with BPD tend to reverse the order in which these two aspects play out in everyday life. Most of us process facts before feelings; yet, individuals with BPD focus on feelings before facts. Moreover, they may actually change the facts in their own minds to match their feelings. If, for example, your loved one has a fear of abandonment (which is quite common for individuals living with BPD), he or she might think that you're walking out on your relationship, even if you're simply going to the grocery store. In order to handle this type of situation, it's in your best interest to try to empathize with your loved one. You might want to say something along the lines of: "I don't want you to be upset. I would be upset, too, if I thought you were leaving for good; however, I'm going grocery shopping and will return in about an hour."

To work on communicating with your loved one, you may also wish to ask questions whenever possible. It might seem counterproductive, but this allows your loved one to feel as if he or she is part of an equal relationship, instead of having to be told "no" all of the time. For example, you can ask for alternative solutions to problems. You might want to say something like, "I can't say yes to this particular situation, but I know that you really want me to. Is there another way we can solve this issue?"

Finally, if you find yourself involved in a conversation or argument that is going nowhere, you might want to use this method to handle it: delay, distract, depersonalize, and detach. First, try to delay the issue by asking your loved one if you can revisit the matter at a later time. Use a calm tone of voice, and tell your loved one that you recognize the importance of the matter, but you need some time to understand it. Next, you can "distract" by suggesting another activity, such as running an errand together. Following that, you'll need to depersonalize the matter. In other words, you can't allow yourself to take any of your loved one's comments personally. Although certain comments might be hurtful, BPD causes people to behave in a way that they normally wouldn't. Finally, you might have to detach yourself from the situation. Distance yourself emotionally from what your loved one is saying or doing in moments of extreme negativity. Tell yourself that you're not going to get caught up in the emotional whirlwind of the situation, and it will help you process everything better. You might also want to do this in moments of extreme positivity as well. For BPD sufferers, things are typically either very positive or extremely unfavorable. By distancing yourself not only from the extreme lows but also from the extreme highs, you'll be less likely to get trapped on a rollercoaster ride of emotions, which will allow you to help your loved one from a clear perspective.

Chapter 10:
How To Keep Sane When Your Loved One Has BPD

Does speaking of retaining sanity look like an attempt at playing victim? Well, it is not. If you are not well informed about Borderline Personality Disorder, you can practically go nuts living with someone with this condition. You can't imagine living in your own home yet you find yourself walking on tip-toe, so to speak, whenever your loved one is around.

Every time you are about to open your mouth to speak you are wondering if what you are going to say is going to upset your partner; even when it is casual talk. And you keep feeling that if you do something you are damned and if you fail to do it you are doomed! Living with someone whose moods you cannot predict and whose moods are always on the extreme can be stressful – enjoying a calm moment now and in the next few moments it is all hell breaking loose with nothing you can pinpoint as an obvious trigger! And at any one time, you are either the angel your loved one cannot live without or the devil who needs to overhaul his or her behavior to fit into your loved one's life.

For a person with BPD, there is no normalcy. And in fact, there is nothing you can do to make such a person see things the way normal people do. Incidentally, if for a moment you doubted if your loved one really was suffering from BPD, your doubts will vanish when you realize that everything that does not please them is your fault – in their eyes, that is. They criticize and blame you even when you cannot see anything amiss yourself or even when you have nothing to do with whatever is amiss. With all this irrational behavior, not to mention the realization that your loved one is undoubtedly bent on manipulating you, it would take extra-ordinary strength or professional intervention for you to remain sane in such a relationship. Can you imagine how much mental power it takes to withstand the fear, the guilt, threats, episodes of violent rage and a lot more outrageous behavior consistently directed at you?

The way experts see it, you need to think about and take care of yourself first before you can be in a position to help your loved one; or even to withstand them and their behavior. The tendency to try and please the person with BPD is an attempt at futility. Your attempts at appeasing them just serve to dry you out of your emotional and physical energy. Ultimately, you are filled with resentment; you are burnt out; and often you fall into depression. Surely, how can you help your loved one if he/she has managed to drive you to the verge of insanity?

Here are some tips experts give:

Mind your welfare

How tempting it is to isolate yourself, feeling overwhelmed by your lack of control and all the negativity from the person closest to you! But make a conscious effort to avoid that. It is imperative that you keep in close touch with your family as well as friends who always made you feel good about you before and still do. You absolutely need to have people in your life that support you and also pay attention to your views; people who appreciate you and who reassure you that you qualify to be cared for. Such are the people who also provide you with some reality check when appropriate.

Have a personal life that does not have to involve your partner

You need to stop feeling guilty about enjoying life as an individual. You surely are not an extension of your partner and you should not permit her or his insecurities to stifle your life. Fight the feeling of guilt that has the tendency of creeping in whenever you begin to enjoy life in any manner. Fun is allowed. You actually deserve it! It helps you relax and rejuvenate. And that way you are in a better position to absorb the irrational talk that comes from your partner who has BPD without feeling like you will lose your mind.

Seek a support group comprised of people like you affected by BPD

Often it helps to mingle with people who are in the same predicament as you are: living with a partner suffering from BPD. Once you share experiences, you cease to blame yourself for non-existent sins attributed to you by your partner. Considering that a good number of people have not come to terms with this condition that is Borderline Personality Disorder, it may be a bit difficult to find such a support group within geographical reach. In that case, you could join an online support group and though you may not meet in person, you can conveniently share your experiences and help each other lead a more fulfilling life.

Take care of your physical health

You need to keep your physical health right by eating healthy as well as regular exercising. You also need to get into the habit of enjoying quality sleep. Mind you if you fail to sleep well, it might get you into mental as well as physical problems, a state you cannot afford to risk with all the drama in your life.

You may not think much of it when you have so many distractions of the firefighting nature, but a healthy, relaxed body and mind are better placed to handle negative behavior as well as extreme emotions such as those you get from your ill partner.

Practice ways of managing your frustration and stress

Do you be think you can always fight fire with fire? Well, not always. Getting mad at your partner who has BPD just to counter their crazy behavior is not the way to earn your sanity. It may actually just aggravate the situation. What you need to do is practice how to manage your sensory input so that you are able to fight agitation and remain calm even as provocation persists.

Get Security from the Rule of 3 Cs

And what is that rule? Well, remember how guilty your partner's constant accusations make you feel – guilty and all? Such accusations cannot but make you wonder what it is you have done wrong. And, unfortunately, it leads you feeling like you are to blame for the destructive behavior of the person with borderline personality disorder. Often you may find yourself justifying the negative behavior of the person and even when they relapse after therapy you may tend to feel like it is your fault. Well, none of that is your fault and you should learn to stop taking undue blame either from your inner self, your partner or anyone else. The three Cs you need to survive by are:

1. I'm not the one who caused this destructive behavior
2. I'm not responsible for curing it
3. It is not in my power to control it

Chapter 11:
Communicate and Behave As Differently As the Person with BPD

A case of fighting fire with fire…? Well, not exactly; but close. In your case, you are being called upon to be realistic about the challenges you face. The fact that you love your partner and you treat them with dignity has not stopped them from treating you badly. Now, you need not hit back by treating them badly – after all, you may not even manage to behave irrationally the way they do even if you wanted – but you need to be realistic that the person you are relating with is not exactly normal.

Practice ignoring remarks and behavior that does not make sense

This may sound, kind of rude, but really, ignoring things that do not make sense in relation to your life is all you do all day long. That is why even when there are thousands of voices in the city streets they do not distract you from conducting your business. You have learnt to sieve them so that you register only that which is relevant and useful to you. Ignoring your partner is not the most natural thing, but for you to survive, this is a skill you need to perfect. Avoid fueling their railing and ranting by giving explanations when you know their raving is irrational.

Leave the chaos

You do not have to sit still and get emotionally tortured by a raving irrational person. Walking away may help the situation for a number of reasons. For one, a person with BPD goes into an illogical tirade because it gives them satisfaction to see you injured; giving them a sense of control over you. So once you leave the scene, your partner will stop her or his tirade for lack of a good target audience. And you will find rescue in a peaceful environment. Tolerating abuse of any nature – be it physical, verbal or even emotional is one of the worst things you could do to yourself.

Keep your language simple

Someone may be tempted to ask: are all people with BPD uneducated? Well, they may as well be very highly educated; but when it comes to this condition, the ability to be logical is highly eroded. Unless they have undergone therapy and understood that they have a medical condition of a mental nature, their level of education does not come into play. So be conscious that their rage can be triggered by a very minor misunderstanding. Therefore, to avoid ambiguity of anything you say – and considering that any misunderstanding is usually for the worse – keep your sentences short and your words simple. Figurative language is not for the people with BPD otherwise you are bound to have hell in your house day in day out, over and above the usual disharmony.

Isolate behavior from the person

It is easy to condemn the person because of the behavior that is so irrational and hurting to you and other people, but you need to try and remind yourself that you have a person with a mental disorder in your life and the disorder needs to be addressed just like you address other ailments like diabetes, hypertension and others. You are not expected to handle this seamlessly as you are a human being too, capable of losing your temper and your patience as well, but you need to keep trying.

Allay their fears in the way that they understand

Why do we keep saying that people with BPD are illogical? Well, lots of reasons; but the bottom line is that they cannot support their behavior with facts the way a normal thinking being does. We have mentioned that people with BPD fear abandonment. So when your BPD wife insists on tagging along when you are going for a boys' outing, remind yourself of her insecurities. Going out without her drives her to believe you will take every opportunity to leave her for good. While the thought may have crossed your mind at some point in your relationship due to continued frustration, this time all you want is to meet your buddies probably for a game or just to hang out. In fact, you are certain that if you were to leave her you would say it to her face and pack your bags.

The best advice is to acknowledge her fears first and say something to reassure her that she is secure with you and that you have no plans of leaving her. Only after that would she be willing to listen to your factual explanation. If you try to reason with her the way you do with people who are mentally healthy – starting your explanation with facts and trying to appease their emotions last or even leaving them to sort out their emotions independently – you will fail at calming the situation.

Avoid being drawn into your partner's emotions

Of course, normally someone would find empathy as something healthy and commendable. However, when you are living with a person whose emotions are borne out of unwarranted fears and panic, it would be harmful for your mental state to take on part of those negative emotions. For you to remain sober, and hopefully be able to calm down your partner, you need to keep your focus on the message. When he or she is raving mad, talk of what happened and how your partner would have loved things to go instead. That way, you will be tempering his or her emotions by evoking some positive thought process; and you will also be protecting yourself from losing your temper and creating a madhouse in the process.

Put the ball in your partner's court

You see, with a person with BPD, the more you try to solve a problem, the more they see the bad side of your solution; and the more they make you feel like the villain. So, to counter that, why not seek solutions from your partner? Ignore the whining and yelling and then calmly inquire from them what they see as the best solution. That way, you are refusing to purport to solve a non-existent problem and letting your partner who claims to be offended suggest a solution.

Be mindful of your timings

There are topics you cannot just broach to your partner, knowing her vulnerability. When it comes to one of you being likely to lose a job, this is a topic you need to handle delicately because your partner with BPD may begin to feel like they are bound to lose you; like you will abandon them because of the negative development. Yet since as someone in your life they need to know what is happening, you need to choose a time when the environment is appropriate; when there is a lot your partner is happy and confident about. People with BPD are not to be updated on things as they happen because their emotions can erupt without warning. They are to be told things at a time well thought out.

Learn and develop skills that neutralize intensity of emotions

By now you, obviously, can visualize a person with BPD flaring with emotions as if ready to tear someone into pieces; or behaving like the skies are about to fall because their needs are not being met right there and then. Since you have no magic wand to wave and quell the chaos, the best you can do is try to keep the 'madness' in check. Experts recommend you use the tactic of the 4 Ds – as in Delay; Distract; Depersonalize; and also Detach.

Here is what each of them really means:

Delaying

Acknowledging that your partner is upset, and not insinuating that they are justified to be upset, try and convince them that you are ready to discuss the reason they are upset and how you can help solve the problem, but only at a later time. Let them feel that you would love it when they are happy. In short, you are buying time for tempers to cool and the 'temporary madness' to subside.

Distracting

Distraction here carries the usual meaning of diverting attention. You want to get your fuming partner's attention from her attention seeking rage to something else. You could ask her, for instance, if both of you could go catch a movie before queues get long; or take kids to fit uniforms; just something to disrupting her unhealthy mindset.

Depersonalizing

What you practice doing here is to divorce your partner from the mental condition he or she bears. Unless you do that, you are bound to get hurt in a way that can even erode your self confidence. The nature of BPD is such that the person suffering it can say things that are very demeaning and cruel.

Detaching

Hey! Don't get exhilarated when a person suffering BPD tells you how much they adore you. Just smile and say thank you – but do not ride the high tide. Before long that high may switch to one of you are the devil who has made their life miserable. In short, you should know better than get emotionally sucked into your partner's intense emotions irrespective of whether they are positive or negative. In fact, you may wish to coin a phrase or a sentence to fall back to every time your partner is on a high of any sort; like, *I'm personally out of this.*

Some people have compared the emotional cycle of a person suffering BPD to a complete row of dominoes. What happens if you push one of those dominoes? Doesn't the entire row come crashing down? In a bid to neutralize the intense emotions of your partner, what you strive to do is push out your own domino. Without your presence, your responses or retorts; your reaction; fuelling the situation, your partner is likely to calm down. One thing that is certain in all your unfortunate episodes is that if you manage to keep your adrenaline stable, you are likely to find it easier to control the situation with your BPD partner. So do your best to keep calm.

Chapter 12:
How to Handle an Employee with BPD

Is Borderline Personality Disorder (BPD) a condition that everyone is familiar with? The answer is a solid no. Some people often categorize people with BPD as crazy, rude, inconsiderate, arrogant… name it. And some of those who have some knowledge about the condition are not prepared to spare time to handle people with BPD in any special way. In many cases, they would rather they pushed them out of their way. Why not trying to blame those who want to give people with BPD a wide berth, it is important to be informed about BPD just in case you find you have a person with the condition amongst your staff. The workplace is where you spend most of your waking hours and you want to be happy when working and not stressed out trying to calm down and reason with illogical, egocentric people. BPD is a condition that cannot be ignored especially when in the US people suffering the condition have hit ten million.

The surprisingly positive side of the working environment for BPD people is that it often provides them a better environment; one where their emotions are often at their most stable. From that you can deduce that when your partner has BPD, they are better actively engaged in something productive than idling around in the house. That is not to say that people with BPD do not cause mayhem for their colleagues at work. They often do because the behavior of a person with BPD is not just erratic but also unpredictable.

What Are The Give-Away Signs That An Employee Has BPD?

The National Association of Mental Illness, abbreviated as NAMI, has a list of symptoms that people with BPD exhibit. Here is how to tell that an otherwise great worker may have BPD:

- The tendency to behave in uncontrolled rage; in great intensity and in a way that is totally inappropriate.

- Exhibiting frequent mood swings that show irritability and anxiety that can go on for long hours or even a couple of days.

- Exhibiting impulsive behavior that is often dangerous; including sex; shoplifting; binge eating; substance abuse; reckless driving among others.

- Incidences of issuing threats to cause injury to themselves or even of a suicidal nature.

- Inter-personal relationships that are extreme as well as intense.

- A tendency to view people in black and white – that means you are either very good or very bad. And as far as experiences go, the person either likes it or detests it; no middle ground.

- Behavior that reflects self doubt as far as self image is concerned; uncertainty regarding the relationships they are in; their long-term goals; and so on.

- Exhibiting an unsettling sign of emptiness and persistent boredom.

- Exhibiting fear that they may be rejected even when there is no pointer towards that direction. Often someone with BPD experiences such fear whenever someone senior to them or even a colleague expresses something that sounds like criticism.

- A tendency to drive other colleagues at loggerheads using malicious gossip which they spread with unparalleled intensity.

Ok – you know that Borderline Personality Disorder is a mental condition and it is usual for people with it to disrupt an otherwise peaceful environment making it chaotic. Are you therefore expected to pave way for these people to cause their havoc and then pick the pieces after them? Are you supposed to handle them with kid gloves or something?

First of all, like they say in some African cultures, you can't succeed in appeasing evil spirits by giving them blood sacrifices – slaughtering animals and feeding the evil spirits with the meat. That is some kind of bribery that doesn't work. If you try it, you realize the winds are calm for just awhile before havoc sets in yet again.

So, here are some practical steps that are helpful in managing the presence of someone with BPD at work:

Remain steadfast in enforcing the rules of your organization and upholding its culture

Just because an employee with BPD may feel like fish out of water if they are new to your culture is no reason for you to alter it; or even to bend rules. You need to actually ensure that all employees understand your organization's etiquette and that the rules guiding how employees carry themselves around are clearly displayed in conspicuous places. Do not accept BPD as an excuse for an employee to abuse or mistreat others at the workplace.

It is important that you even take time to admonish any employee you notice is being disrespectful to another. And when you do it in private, the message tends to get home better without that employee feeling humiliated. The way you deliver your warning should be such that the employee will understand that you care equally for each one of their lot and that all you want is peace and harmony at the workplace. And doing it in private also helps you to understand the thinking of individual employees and their attitude. And it is during these interactions, more than any other time at work that you are likely to identify any employee suffering from Borderline Personality Disorder.

But as already mentioned, the advantage of knowing whoever has BPD is not so that you can exonerate them from any wrongdoing – far from it. It is so that you can see how such employees can be helped through therapy; affiliations to certain helpful social groups; and even by making other employees understand the BPD condition and its implications.

Handle incidences of disruption with an open mind

Fight the temptation to dash to conclusions when you find friction between or amongst your employees. Try to understand the whole picture; that is including the genesis of the argument or discord. You may come to learn that what caused a whole production line to stop or get messed up was a minor remark or such other trivial matter. Remember what may seem minor to an average person does not appear minor to someone with personal insecurities. Since not all arguments and misunderstandings occur due to the involvement of someone with BPD, yours is to try and reconcile the antagonizing parties and helping them back to a state where they can work in harmony.

In case further misunderstandings occur on the same working zone, it will be a pointer to you that there is a significant problem in your workplace that needs serious addressing. For starters, you could separate the warring parties so that they do not work in the same groups or the same production line. Beyond that it may be a good idea to formulate some actionable measures involving the affected employees. It may even be time for you to pay for some teambuilding sessions for your entire workforce, whatever modalities you put in place. In order for your business to succeed, your employees must work in harmony; and discord cannot be entertained even when a person with BPD is involved, without an attempt at rectifying the situation.

Employees' morale is paramount if you are to keep your business growing at a respectable rate and it only thrives when everyone around is happy. That means if you have to take drastic steps like restructuring your whole workforce to keep employees' morale up, then you need to go ahead and do it.

Acknowledge the strengths of the person with BPD

Did we mention somewhere that a person with BPD can be very productive at work? It means then that there is something good you can tap from such a person for the benefit of the organization. Long before the eruptive spells emerge, or even after they have come and gone, point out the good contribution the person brings to your organization. You can do that in public and in private as well.

Of course you must remember the emphasis we have put on the weakness that a person with BPD has – mainly that of feeling rejected. This, often, is the root of a lot of mess that the person causes when working with others. With the information you now have, you are in a position to pre-empt those destructive episodes or at least reduce them. One way of doing that is having a conversation with the affected employee, regarding her or his role in the department and the organization as a whole. Let them know that their contribution is important to the organization. And no – you aren't trying to flatter them because in the course of your private conversation, you are also going to explain the role the employee's colleagues also play. That then makes it explicit that each one of them has an important role that is not in competition with that of someone else.

Now, what is the impact of such detailed discussions? Well, for one, the person develops a good level of trust in you. And, of course, trust fights fear. The employee knows how you feel about them; that you are not about to recommend their sacking; so they are bound to suppress any fear trying to grip them whenever other people perform well in their respective duties. Again there is clarity in the person's mind where he or she stands with the organization and that elevates the feeling of security. Or rather, it fights off the ever creeping fear of being rejected. Ultimately, the reassurance that the person is valued and the strengthened feeling of security serve to produce calmness. Needless to say, calmness and harmony are fundamental requirements if you are to enjoy a healthy working atmosphere.

Encourage any employee with BPD to seek professional help

Have we said anywhere in this chapter that a manager can solve problems of BPD? No! What any person in a position of leadership can do is guide all employees in a manner to quell or reduce misunderstandings; do whatever it takes to motivate them; and create the best working environment in his or her power. Beyond that you can only recommend a struggling employee whom you suspect has BPD to see a doctor or a professional counselor.

If the organization has an Employee Assistance Program, encourage your employee to check in and seek help. This is a good move as you cannot expect your employees to spill all the problems they have to you or any other senior, including those of a private nature. Yet you are aware that some of the anger you see manifested at the workplace is triggered by things happening at home. In fact, this is the point where you bring out all options; including a suggestion that the employee joins a support group. If you are really convinced that what you are dealing with is a case of BPD, you can even go the extra mile and check out some good support groups, even online, and then give the employee the contacts.

Chapter 13:
Simple Changes for a Happier Life

When you're living with someone who has a mental illness, there are going to be good days and bad days. Yet, you can make things easier overall and keep the bad days from becoming even worse by following a few tips, which are listed below.

First of all, understand that when someone is coping with a mental illness such as narcissistic personality disorder or BPD, bad days *will* come. Unfortunately, that's just a fact and an inevitable part of living with a mental illness. Yet, if you recognize them and accept bad days for what they are, it can be easier for you to cope with them. Don't meet them with resistance; rather, accept them and approach them with calm understanding as much as you can.

If you had plans to do something on a day in which your loved one is struggling, you may have to postpone or cancel your original plans. That's where communicating with friends and family members can work to your advantage: if they already know what you and your loved one are struggling with, they'll be more inclined to react in an understanding manner when you need to adjust plans.

Also, if things truly get out of hand, don't be afraid to seek outside help. Hopefully, your loved one has already agreed to seek help from a qualified mental health expert. Nonetheless, there may still be incidents that require immediate medical attention. Especially for individuals with BPD, suicidal thoughts can become frequent and debilitating. If your loved one is seriously considering committing suicide or makes an attempt, hospitalization may be necessary. Don't view this as a defeat; it's what may be required for your loved one to get past this very difficult time.

For some couples, hospitalizations or treatment programs offer an ideal solution. While the loved one struggling with the mental illness finds help, the other partner gets a bit of a break. While hospitalization isn't always necessary and shouldn't be used in place of therapy, it can act as relief for you while your partner is suffering: you'll know that he or she is safe, and that for the time being, his or her care is out of your hands.

While your loved one seeks counseling and sets out on the journey towards wellness, it should be your goal to educate yourself as much as possible about his or her mental illness. Your loved one's psychologist or psychiatrist might provide resources that you can use to inform yourself, such as pamphlets or websites. You can also check in with your library to find reference books with detailed information about the illness and coping strategies.

In addition, you should seek a support group for your own benefit, as well. After all, as a support system and partner of a person who's living with a mental illness, you're bound to feel bogged down from time to time. The responsibility, patience, and understanding you'll need to maintain are far greater than what most individuals typically offer in relationships. You may want to seek counseling on your own; or, perhaps you should consider looking into online forums. You can become a member and find a support system online made up of many other people who know what you're going through and have struggled through the same issues firsthand.

It may also benefit you to fully recognize your loved one's limitations. Try to avoid putting your loved one in potentially difficult situations. For example, if your loved one is experiencing high levels of anxiety, don't put him or her in a situation that will make it worse, such as forcing him or her to attend a social outing. Even if it's important to you, you may have to do some compromising at this point in your relationship.

Finally, remember that tough love will be essential throughout this journey. If you refuse to stay strong on certain issues, you'll allow the cycle of negativity to continue. Your loved one may try to convince you that seeking help is unnecessary, or that he or she doesn't need to continue therapy sessions. In reality, you may be a better judge of your loved one's mental state, since you come from an outside perspective yet still know him or her very well. You must be prepared to be firm, but loving, and recognize the fact that you'll need to hold your loved one accountable for the actions required to achieve mental wellness. Your commitment to maintaining a sense of tough love is crucial to your relationship, and to the betterment of your loved one's mental state.

Chapter 14:
Anything Good You Can Reap From The Narcissist?

It will not be surprising if you are waiting with bated breath and hoping for a positive answer here, because clearly, just reading through the chapters and visualizing life with a narcissist is enough to make your world cloudy. And you cannot fail to sympathize with anyone living with a narcissist or working with one. After all, who is this who has capacity to endlessly give without getting anything in return and with no hope of ever getting a reprieve? Surely dominance; hostility; and even arrogance are not dishes you would order even if they had the least price on the menu. Yet that is what the narcissist in your life brings to your table whether you like it or not.

Having seen how difficult it is to change the behavior of a narcissist considering it is equally difficult to get them to seek professional help, you will, no doubt, count your lucky stars if someone can show you any bright side to having a narcissist around. As the saying goes, necessity is the mother of invention. Someone must have seen the pain borne out of relating with narcissists and analyzed things to see what good the world can get from this same person who has no empathy for anyone. Let us say, there is an element or two of narcissism that can be deemed healthy and those ones you can tap into and benefit your organization.

Here is how your organization can benefit from having a narcissistic leader:

Narcissists are able to focus on the vision

As long as the narcissism is not extreme, narcissist leaders are able to focus on the company vision because they like being associated with success. And the better if they hope to share the credit, if not singularly bear it. Incidentally, such people can even create a vision even where none existed because that in itself makes them catch attention. Narcissists, as you know do love attention. A leader with a healthy level of narcissism is able to see the broad picture as far as the growth of the company is concerned.

Narcissists can be great at mobilizing

Do you remember us saying that narcissists love to be admired? Well, they are often not disappointed because there are many people who are drawn to people who are outgoing; and many narcissists are in that category of outgoing people. Now, with their ability to attract a sizeable following, narcissists can do well to get people to rally behind a proposal; a policy; a political party; the like. Do not forget that narcissists are good at articulating what they need and what they expect of you. And since they are usually good at oral skills as well and charisma often comes with it, your narcissistic leader may be just what the doctor ordered in particular times.

Narcissists can be successful in building business empires

Since the narcissist is desirous of gaining attention and is very eager about it, they can easily focus their energies towards building a successful business that makes people's heads turn. And, of course, the hope is that all and sundry will know that they are the brains behind the success. Do not be surprised to see the narcissistic entrepreneur building a series of businesses as long as they can. One positive aspect of this is that even as they contribute positively to the exchequer, they also do a lot of good creating employment for other people. Don't other employers engage employees as well, you may wonder?

Of course, they do. But with a narcissist, the more subordinates he or she engages, the better for the ego. And so the narcissist may not do too much cost-benefit analysis like other employers. To the narcissist the more pertinent question would be who can give me a salute for giving them employment? And the longer the queue – and the number of people saluting – the more satisfying it is for the narcissistic leader.

They are great at handling situations that call for coldness

Not that anyone is advocating for ruthlessness or anything of the kind, but sometimes leaders are faced with extremely difficult situations that need tough action. Take the case of a retrenchment program, especially where the employees have not been well prepared for it. An empathetic leader may find it a very trying moment to have to terminate the services of employees who have been loyal to the company and who have great financial responsibilities to bear.

But come your narcissist leader and getting people off the payroll and dishing out termination letters is like a delicious cup of coffee. What is there to think about, anyway? Financial responsibilities...? Whose problem is that? To the narcissist, everything can go as technical and as matter-of-fact as can be without the slightest feeling. In the circumstances, the narcissistic leader is the competent executor of policies that management is glad to have. And in countries where labor unions are not very strong, the narcissist is the darling of employers. That's the guy to tell the employees when they start grumbling about low salaries and wages – take it or leave it. And that is, without batting an eyelid even when the pay is abhorrent.

They are often great in competitions

To narcissists, winning draws the limelight onto them. So whatever it takes – drilling, practice or whatever – they can commit themselves to it just to come out shining over everyone else. Of course, you will love the narcissist to be on your team at such times. However, as you may already know, the narcissist may be tempted to cut a few corners in order to make the win. But since your conscience will not allow you to play foul and you have the narcissist who has no conscience, anyway, your team will be well taken care of.

So what do you learn in this chapter? Well, the narcissist, with all the ill feelings that the reference elicits, can have attributes that you can tap into for the benefit of everyone else around. This chapter has simply demonstrated the art of separating the wheat from the chaff. For example, for the lack of empathy, do not for whatever reason entrust the narcissist with mentoring. That would be like condemning an employee with potential to hell in the name of mentorship. You surely do not want to witness the narcissist trying to make a version of himself or herself out of his or her protégé.

And do not make them in charge where brainstorming is required. If you do, they are going to shut down everyone and try to push their own ideas down everyone's throat. How fruitful, really, would be the results of such a session? Besides having a great desire to shine and dominate you are aware narcissists are also not capable of listening. That is a clear minus where you want the benefit of diverse ideas. Yet you have seen there is a lot more good you could tap from this same narcissist.

Chapter 15:
Handling a Narcissist without Losing Control of Your Emotions

Seriously... is that possible? How does someone milk you dry, use you to climb the ladder of success and all while ignoring your needs, and on realizing the exploitation be expected to handle the situation calmly like some light wind just blew past? This might sound like too much, of course considering you are also human; in fact a human being more sensitive than your narcissistic partner or colleague, but the truth is that getting all worked up and possibly engaging in heated verbal exchange does not do much, if anything at all, to help.

So how do you do this calm handling of the narcissist amidst all the provocation? Well, you need first to identify what kind of narcissist you are dealing with? Oops! So there are narcissists and other narcissists...? Alright! Actually experts in the field of psychology have done significant amount of research regarding this mental disorder that is narcissism. And a number of them, including Vincent Egan from the University of Nottingham and his colleagues, have established there are variations of narcissists each of whom behaves differently to some extent. Here are two common types of narcissists:

1. **Vulnerable narcissist**
2. **Grandiose narcissist**

Vulnerable Narcissist

Did we say that a narcissist has no feelings? Well, it may come across that way, but what they really lack is empathy. They couldn't care less whether you felt pain, disappointment or excitement. All they care is about your response to their feelings. Crazy, we would say, if it were not for the fact that narcissism is a mental disorder.

What actually makes a vulnerable narcissist stand out is their high level of emotional sensitivity particularly when you do not treat them in a manner to suggest they are royalty. It is like they hunger for affirmation. So in such times, they suffer from a feeling of helplessness and they get extremely anxious. Vulnerable narcissists are perennially worrying about the possibility of being rejected or abandoned.

Then again, there is another unsettling aspect of being a vulnerable narcissist. The person may be charged this moment and very low the next. This fluctuation of emotions swings from one of superiority to one of inferiority. So if you are thinking of curative methods for such a person, you can see what a challenge you would be facing. Just to make things clearer, take an instance where the vulnerable narcissists deeply believes there is a great chance of being divorced; or even losing a job. If at such a time you advice them to see a counselor or a therapist to help them through those fears, you will be surprised at how they will shoot and religiously attend the therapy sessions. But don't hold your breath. That consistency only last for the period when the threat looks real and the fear is intense. Sooner or later your vulnerable narcissist will call it a day even before the recommended period of therapy is up. They just drop out without apologies.

With your vulnerable narcissist, the meanness you see is a way of compensating – though theirs really is over-compensating – for possible low self esteem and probably deep seated shame that began very early in age. It is possible that such a person was neglected as a child or even abused, and over time he or she has developed a way of coping with the negative experience. As grown-ups, vulnerable narcissists strive to gain respect while at the same time they cannot stomach any feedback that suggests they alter their behavior albeit a little bit. And as a partner you are wondering – how do I speak in superlatives about this person who is not ready to appreciate an objective assessment from someone who genuinely cares?

Grandiose Narcissist

Grandiose narcissists feel superior to everyone else. Chances are that they got used to being treated special and in a manner to suggest they were better than other people when they were children. As such they have developed that expectation of being treated like they were superior to all other people. Grandiose narcissists are one confident lot who, nevertheless, cannot digest negative feedback. And like the vulnerable narcissist, they also hunger for attention and praise; only that these ones fall into a rage whenever the kind of respect and attention they long for is not forthcoming. The grandiose narcissists have high self esteem and that is a good thing. What overshadows that good attribute, however, is their lack of empathy – their insensitivity to the feelings of other people.

Have you heard of people with Anti-social Personality Disorder (ASPD)? Well, these ones are a lot that is very difficult to cope with in the community. And unfortunately, the grandiose narcissist has some shared behavior with these people, including the tendency to be aggressive and domineering; as well as lacking in remorse whenever they are alerted about incidences of insensitivity towards other people.

Now you know how each of the two variants of narcissists behaves. How do you deal with them without feeling like you are on a roller coaster ride?

First establish what 'breed' of narcissist you are dealing with

Once you know the kind of narcissist you are dealing with, you will know the kind of roles that suit them if there are responsibilities to be undertaken whether at work, among family members or even as friends. You know if there are things to be done outdoors or even indoors but involving many people, your grandiose narcissist is your best bet. You just need to spell out your goals and your grandiose will push everyone until what needs to be done gets done. As for your vulnerable narcissist, you clearly will do well to fit them behind the scenes or where they will not need to worry what others think of his or her performance – at least not in public.

Let it be known when the narcissist is getting on your nerves

After you have identified the type of narcissist you are dealing with, you can know the effective way to reduce their interference and probably even get them to make positive contribution. If you bottle your frustration inside, beware that you risk exploding at the most unexpected moment – and that is neither good for you nor for the narcissist.

Get to note the narcissist who is being a nuisance

What would you do if you noted a vulnerable narcissist making mischief in the middle of a serious tutorial session, for instance? Simple, first of all you know the reason the vulnerable narcissist makes mischief is to gain recognition because deep down he or she believes that nobody can take notice of them under normal circumstances. So, how about identifying one of the narcissist's good qualities and bring it up, albeit as a by-the-way?

You could even mention some nice contribution this narcissist had made earlier on. With that affirmation that they are good and worth recognition, your vulnerable narcissist will not find reason to continue making mischief. You see – you have not lost your temple, you have not humiliated your vulnerable narcissist, and the session is back on track.

And if you realize your culprit is a grandiose narcissist, why not give them a challenge? You could even get them to chair the session while you watch and follow. By so doing you will be providing them with the feeling that brings out their best – you give them recognition and they, in turn, do their best to prove to everyone that they can meet the challenge.

Understand the context

There are times a person's insecurities are aroused because of the situation. If so, you may wish to put the narcissist in a different environment. Take for instance a case where two colleagues who have been working closely submit their applications for promotion and one of them gets it while the other one does not. If the one who missed the promotion is a vulnerable narcissist, that miss may serve to affirm to them that they are inadequate. As such, they may not work well with the colleague with whom they sought promotion. In such circumstances, you could choose to shift the vulnerable narcissist to a section where he or she will not have to work directly under or even with that other colleague. If you do not remedy the situation, you are likely to be faced with an employee who is spiteful and also vindictive. So you have studied your people, identified the narcissists and known what category they belong to, and you have used that information to keep the running smooth.

Keep feeling positive and showing it

If you are particularly dealing with the grandiose narcissist who relishes the feeling of superiority at the expense of others, do not respond with pain and anguish when they step on your toes. And when next they get talking to them, address them like you had been too naïve to realize they were provoking you. Once they realize you are not the type to satisfy their longing to domineer, coax and coerce, they will stop that irritating behavior. In fact, they will not wish to subject themselves further to being ignored.

Let your sense of humor do wonders for you

Suppose instead of ignoring the unbecoming behavior, as in number above, you simply laugh off the provocation of the grandiose narcissist? You could point out clearly but lightheartedly how absurd or inappropriate the narcissist's behavior was. Here the grandiose narcissist will take note, but because you did not help inflate his or her ego, very likely you will not see a repeat of that behavior.

Chapter 16:
Treatment for People with BPD

What kind of treatment do you imagine the doctor or therapist prescribes for a person with BPD? Of course you are right if you reckon there is no one prescription that suits everyone. Different people calling in for medical attention under the banner of BPD often manifest different symptoms. Some may be chaotic at home with physical aggression marking their day; others may just be incessant whiners that can drive people around insane; and others have every symptom you can imagine, starting from verbal abuse to threats of self-harm.

Since BPD is mainly a defect of a behavioral nature, therapists mostly tend to begin with talk therapy before any other form of treatment. Generally when you take the person to the therapist, expect a prescription of two weekly sessions. The therapist capable of helping a person with BPD is one qualified to handle matters of mental health. Apart from establishing that the therapist is qualified, you also need to establish that your person is comfortable being attended by the particular therapist. If the two are not comfortable with each other, there is no way the therapy sessions can be effective.

Do all people with BPD take the same time to get well?

No, different people with BPD may take different periods of time for the symptoms of the condition to go away, and there are those symptoms that are more difficult to alleviate than others.

Among the symptoms that respond well to treatment include anger; attempts at self harm as well as suicide; adjusting to different social environments. Those that are pretty difficult to deal with include fear of abandonment; the feeling of sheer emptiness; instability of relationships; and such. Then there is, of course, the danger of recurrence of symptoms. Someone who seems to have improved can begin to show signs of depression and may even relapse into substance abuse; kinds of eating disorders; or even suffer post traumatic stress disorder. Fear of remission should, however, not deter you from getting help for the person with BPD. According to experts, even when people relapse, they hardly become as bad as they were before.

Here are the commonest treatments for BPD:

DBT – Dialectical Behavioral Therapy

This form of therapy is considered the most effective in treating complication of BPD. It involves a pro-active approach to treatment. It is one of those methods that was designed primarily with BPD in mind, and not just a method adopted from another area of treatment.

DBT focuses on the mindset of the person with BPD as it addresses the prevailing emotions. It teaches specific skills that help to deal with intense emotions and generally manage episodes of distress. What the therapist seeks to achieve is a good balance between being able to accept certain behavior and being able and ready to adjust certain behavior. The way DPT is conducted includes one on one as well as group sessions; and sometimes, when necessary, phone sessions.

CBT – Cognitive Behavior Therapy

This is one form of therapy where there is an attempt to make the person with BPD view situations the way other people do; that is normal and not threatening. It works on the person's beliefs and the way they react to situations based on inaccurate conclusions. On the overall, CBT helps the person with BPD to have fewer episodes of anxiety and also to experience reduced mood swings. It also serves to improve the person's perception of other people and themselves too.

MBT – Mentalization Based Therapy

This is another form of talk therapy, whereby the therapist gets the person with BPT to understand how other people feel about their behavior. As they discuss the person's behavior, they also make the person have a good idea what other people think about it.

TFP – Transference Focused Therapy

Here the therapist uses his or her relationship with the person with BPD as an example. The two try and see exactly how emotions erupt and how those emotions affect each other and how ultimately a relationship is affected. Once the patient sees firsthand how actions and behavior affect a relationship, they feel motivated to apply that knowledge to other different relationships. And it proves to be a great way of having the person re-think and adjust behavior in other different situations.

Medication

Taking medication is not a guaranteed solution when it comes to BPD. What it helps to tone down are some conditions that come together with this mental condition. So the doctor may find it worthwhile to prescribe medication aimed at reducing the seriousness of depression; or even the intensity of anxiety or impulsivity. One thing you need to know is that some of those medications have negative side effects and you need to initiate the discussion about them if the doctor says nothing about them. Generally, no medication has been confirmed to cure BPD, but Omega 3 Fatty Acids, which have been seen to relieve symptoms like those of aggression as well as depression, may be helpful.

Self Care

If you want to reduce the negative impact of BPD, try as much as possible to lead a healthy life. This means you eat well in relation to a balanced diet; you adhere to quality sleeping habits; you take your medication as per the doctor's prescription; and you avoid putting yourself in situations whose stressful nature is obvious. When you mind how you lead your life, chances are that your moods will cease to fluctuate uncontrollably, and you will find yourself becoming less impulsive and irritable. In short, take care of your overall health and the symptoms of BPD will dissipate.

Chapter 17:
Tips for a Family with a Person with BPD

How is a family expected to cope with a person with Borderline Personality Disorder? Remember you do not become family by choice. In fact as a family member you are in a very different position from that of a colleague or a neighbor. The latter two can decide to give the person with BPD a wide berth by different means – changing jobs; renting an apartment further away; refusing them entry into their home; lots of choices. But if you are family you are stuck with the person for better or worse. Matters of consanguinity cannot be altered.

That is why it is important that you understand how to behave around someone with BPD and also how to treat them in a constructive way, because you can never be sure if you will come to identify someone with BPD in your family. In any case, you may know about your blood relations today, but you cannot be certain who will become family by marriage; and the people in their lives.

Here are some tips you will find handy:

Avoid talking of great progress

Do you want your relation to get well? Of course, yes – and fast if possible. Even then, you are being warned against verbalizing the progress as you see it when it is impressive. Now – make no mistake. If someone is improving, sustaining calm for long spells or for days, it is worth a mention. But the way you communicate that matters a lot. The positive way of doing this is by saying something to the effect that you know

> Ask what they are doing that has helped? ID the behaviors - Do more of it.

the journey to recovery is tough; but you can see the person is on the right track. Then encourage them to keep doing what they are doing and slowly by slowly they will feel better.

What professionals do not want you doing is exclaiming how great the progress is; things to the effect that nobody would ever tell the person had challenges and so forth. The reason...? Well, in the mind of a person with BPD, saying anything that insinuates that they are as good as healed is tantamount to saying I see no need to keep assisting you and you can do everything on your own now without my attention. Isn't that not what triggers panic in people with BPD – anything that signals the potential for abandonment? In fact, if you go on about how improved the person has become, it may just be a matter of days before you begin to see signs of the old self. The person is likely to panic and begin to raise issues that call for personal attention – call it a relapse.

Some of the regression that has been witnessed when people undergoing therapy for BPD get scared of progress manifests in missing work; over-indulging in eating or even drinking; self mutilation; and even attempted suicide. These are not calculated moves but natural reaction driven by the mental condition that is BPD. This degree of regression is really bad because you may have no choice but to have the family member hospitalized. And what happens when such a person is hospitalized? Well, the person is back to full dependence – the dependence that gives them the attention persons with BPD yearn for. You surely do not want to slide back to that point. So, the message here, in short, is: handle matters of the person's progress with care. Temper the way you speak of their progress because to them, progress denotes abandonment.

Tone down your expectations

When as a family you are happy the member of your family who suffers from Borderline Personality Disorder has accepted to go for therapy, and you get excited that they have shown signs of progress, refrain from making an ambitious list of things-to-do for them. Of course, after getting better the person can complete their degree if they had stalled midway; they can run their own business; they can build a great career; and they can do lots of other great things. But if such a list would overwhelm you who suffer not from such a mental condition, what makes you think the person recovering from BPD would handle it well? In day to day life, when people keep saying how good you are and the range of things they believe you can accomplish, sometimes you begin to feel the pressure. Gladly, you are mentally healthy so you don't take it out on anyone and you don't resort to behavior that is self destructing. The reality is that what puts you under pressure does it a hundredfold for a person with BPD.

The advice to family and friends is to cease stipulating multiple high expectations for the person recovering from BPD. In fact, refrain from talking of long term goals in relation to this person – it can be overwhelming. And once a person is overwhelmed, they get discouraged and that automatically spells failure. So instead of ambitious plans and long-term goals, encourage the person to pursue one thing at a time.

Wait a minute – does it mean we should ignore the person's strengths?

Of course, not! Having BPD does not imply that the person lacks in intellect; artistic talent; inner and outer beauty; ambition; name it. And there is no suggestion that these strengths should be ignored. But as you have already learnt from earlier chapters, BPD makes the person's vulnerabilities overshadow her or his strengths.

So while trying to help and encourage the person to shine in her or his strengths, family members need to be cautious not to put the person on dangerous grounds. And by dangerous grounds we mean a position of vulnerability. If you push the person to try this and that just because you believe they can – and maybe they actually can – if they end up performing second best it might make them feel like they have let you down; let themselves down; and have totally failed. Now, that is the reason pressure is best avoided and high expectations toned down.

Without set expectations, an athlete, for example, recovering from BPD would be encouraged if they made it in the Top 10 in a long distance race. On the contrary, with the family having expressed their high expectations, making it to the Top 10 but failing to clinch a medal might translate to failure in the mind of the athlete. And such are the disappointments that easily cause a relapse. What experts recommend apart from toning down your expectations is splitting a long term goal into short term goals that are easily achievable. Achieving each of these goals boosts the person's self confidence; encourages them; and throws unnecessary fears out of the window.

Let moderation be your guide

Do you get excited when things are going great for you in life? You definitely, do, don't you? And you are bound to get excited as well when people you care about succeed in their endeavors. However, when it comes to a family member with the weaknesses occasioned by BPD, you don't want to get too excited in a manner that they feel the pressure to keep up the success. As we mentioned earlier on, if you show them too much excitement and then they fall short in delivery, they are bound to feel like total failures and lapse into their self destructive state. By the same vein, you will be putting unwarranted pressure on the family member with BPD if you keep expressing your fear that they may not succeed.

We are reminded by experts that people with BPD withstand stress that comes with criticism; rejection; and other equally intense challenges. For that reason, you need to be encouraging calmness when relating with such a person, and even when it comes to giving compliments, you need to keep them tempered just the same way you need to keep your criticism tempered. The three elements that you need to take as a guide as far as the emotions of a person with BPD goes are Affect Decontrol; Intolerance of Aloneness; and also the person's Black And White Thinking.

Affect Dyscontrol

This simply means that this person close to you is not in a position to control his or her emotions. If it is feeling of anger, when it skyrockets, the person seems to sail with the tide rising both in intensity and in the volume of voice that manifests it.

One thing you need to understand is that a person with BPD does not feel emotions that are unique or strange – no. They are feelings that you also experience one time or another. For instance, if you were filling an official form manually and then you realize you have put your signature where your full name was supposed to be, you want to hit yourself in disgust. You could even panic especially if there was a deadline to be met in submitting the form. The difference between you and a person with BPD is that in such circumstances, you do not fall into a rage and tear up the form in frustration. You may find yourself remarking, well, I'll submit the form as it is and whoever is reviewing the form should be able to tell what belongs where – it's no big deal. Or you may decide, ok, I just have to request for another form and fill it afresh. In short, your period of frustration passes quickly; and everyone can understand why for a moment you were upset.

However, with a person suffering BPD, you can never tell what will make their emotions rise and how long those intense emotions are going to last. Sometimes the person's emotions can change a couple of times in a single day without any obvious reason. Again, people with BPD tend to be unable to see alternatives to a problem often dwelling on the worst that could be.

Inability to tolerate being alone

Who doesn't miss another person with whom they have been associating for a significant duration? Surely none – missing a friend, an acquaintance, a coach, a teacher, when they go on long vacation is quite normal. However, you don't let that feeling adversely affect your life to the extent that you become, kind of, dysfunctional. You are capable of reminding yourself that the person you are missing is only going to be away for a while and will be back. The problem with people with BPD is that their memory of good things and security does not seem to serve them well. So the temporary departure of someone they are used to relying on translates to abandonment. Needless to say, the thought of abandonment triggers intense negative emotions of anger and panic among others.

Thinking in plain black and white

This black and white expression attributed to people with BPD means that they do not appreciate that every person has a good and bad; a weak and strong; and such other contrasting sides – that no normal person is perfect just as nobody is entirely evil. Experts term this way of thinking Dichotomous Thinking. Owing to this inability to give room for a person's weaknesses and also room to see a person's goodness, people with BPD have this tendency of grouping attributes into two extremes – evil versus angelic.

Anyone being asked how they would wish a person with BPD to view them might be tempted to say it is good to be seen as extremely good. But what you may not realize, unless, of course, you have read facts as those provided in a book like this one, is that whenever you exhibit caring tendencies and are supportive, the person takes you to be their savior. And what's wrong with that you may wonder – plenty. It means then that you cannot afford to take a break from chores that bring you mingling with this person because, if you do, the person will take that as abandonment. And again you have no freedom to oppose anything they say or disapprove of anything they do. When you do something like that – a normal thing amongst people with no mental issues – the person with BPD takes that to mean you to be uncaring and actually evil. In short, a person with BPD, experiences extremely intense emotions and following those emotions their thinking becomes extreme as well.

Keep to family routines

The point being made here is that you should be alive to the reality that coming home to be with family including the person who keeps upsetting others is not anyone's cup of tea. You are likely to give all manner of excuses just to avoid the toxic environment usually created by the behaviour of the person with BPD.

And there is another reason why family members isolate themselves; not just from the person with BPD but also from the larger society. Mental conditions are usually stigmatizing. The big question is: Does any wrong come out of this manner of isolation? And the answer is in the affirmative. The entire family suffers in one way or another following this kind of isolation. For one, trying to conceal a problem, like in this case trying to hide the existence of a relative with BPD can be exhausting. And it often causes anxiety as you can never tell when the stigmatizing news is going to leak.

At the same time, family time is essential to reinforcing unity, which in turn gives every family member a sense of security. And people get to relax in an environment where people are genuine in whatever they say be it giving compliments or criticism. It is the kind of environment that helps to cool down any tension that may have built over time owing to the stress of dealing with the member with BPD. So essentially, we are saying that family routines are helpful to every member of the family including the person with BPD.

Bring up neutral and light discussions

If you think you are the only one exhausted by the impact of this mental condition that is BPD, you are out of touch. Other family members suffer the same fate and the person who has the conditions is often overwhelmed. This condition and many other ailments are often beyond the power of the ill person to control; so we cannot ask why the person cannot help everyone else by behaving well. The triggers of anger and frustration often work in a way close to how steroids do – making one behave uncontrollably; like there is an overwhelming force behind the reactions.

In short, everyone in the family can do with a break every now and then. You appreciate there is a problem in the family and it is adversely affecting normalcy; so try and create that normalcy. Schedule family dinner times or such other family time where no-one brings up the topic of BPD or anything related to it. You will find yourselves laughing and bonding in a healthy ways you hardly enjoy in your daily lives. That is also good for the person with BPD as they get to shift their minds off their mental condition that seems to define their day-to-day life.

Of course, with clinic to attend, support groups to engage with, spells of emotional upheaval; little else is left for the person with BPD to think about but the condition. But if you think about it critically, suffering a health condition of one form or another does not dilute the fact that you are a human being with natural talents and personal wishes as far as life goals are concerned. And it is during such periods of relaxation that the positive thoughts of what you can do come to mind and you get to share with other family members. This can bring great relief to the family – seeing a positive side of you if you are the one with BPD; and not just associating you with introducing and catalyzing tensions. Once you manage to keep to these relaxing family schedules, sooner or later you may realize you no longer need timetables. Instead you naturally find yourselves seeking each other out to socialize and relax. This enhances healthy relationships amongst yourselves, and of great importance, between the person suffering BPD and the rest of you.

Listen to criticisms even when they are unwarranted

Yes, we said listen – not admit to them! You know what you will be effectively doing? You are letting the person with BPD vent out his or her anger, which as you already know erupts uncontrollably. The advice you need to take away from here is that you need to fight the urge to explain yourself to the person in a defensive manner. Is it nice listening to false accusations? No, it isn't! It hurts. But since you have all your mental faculties in place, and you are well informed after reading such material as contained in this book, you can bring yourself to keep calm.

As you may already have experienced in your daily interaction with this person, trying to explain your innocence only serves to increase the person's venom; and you may never see the end to the verbal barrage. After all, the person with BPD translates your defense as an accusation about them getting annoyed for no good reason – and the person cannot stomach such an allegation. You see, with a person with BPD, you do not have to literally say something accusing or make an accusation like the one your person sees in this case. Such a person's mind is already set to conjure up negative conclusions.

However, what you do in cases where you know there is an element of truth in the person's accusations but the person is only exaggerating its seriousness, you can respond by saying you understand the person has a basis for getting upset and that you are sorry you upset them. What actually complicates handling of a person with BPD as far as anger is concerned is that while the mental condition may be exacerbating the situation, the person may also have been born with the trait of aggressiveness. Natural aggressiveness coupled with a form of mental imbalance cannot make a good recipe.

Pay attention to threats of a destructive nature

Experts say you cannot afford to ignore threats that a person with BPD issues. Often they threaten to harm themselves and you would not like a situation where the person makes a threat, you ignore it, and then the person ends up making good the threat. However, what you need to guard against is giving the threats too much attention lest the person begins to revel at the attention. Someone once told of an incident where a parent called an ambulance in panic when the daughter with BPD made threats and was at the verge to doing something harmful to herself. On the way to the hospital, the teenager's mind switched from her aggravation to reveling at the opportunity to ride in an ambulance – and, of course, the fact that she was the center of attention at that particular moment must have been something she cherished.

You are encouraged as a family not to fear broaching the subject of illness before your affected member. It may be difficult thinking of the possibility of a loved one having a mental ailment, but it is even harder bringing yourself to talk about it. But discussing the issue is the first step to solving the challenges of living with a person with BPD. Expect the person to get upset at the whole idea just as you should expect them to urge you to keep your nose of their life. Besides, if your affected family member is an adult they may invoke the reality of right to privacy. Possibly the most sensitive thing is bringing up the idea that one of you is mentally sick. With the stigma that is associated with mental illness, you may receive opposition, not just from the affected individual, but also from other members of the family.

The most important thing you could do is help the person come to terms with the reality that they have a problem that they need help dealing with. Once you have managed to do that, it becomes relatively easier to tone down triggers that provoke the person into a rage; and you are also better placed to handle the tantrums, whining and such other irritating behaviour. On the overall, if you can pre-empt the person's episodes of raving or even water their impact, you can avert a lot of trouble and bring some peace in the home.

Pre-empt destructive behaviour by listening

As a relative dealing with someone with BPD, how do you feel when you listen to the person expressing views that you feel are outrageous; like saying how you despise them or how little you think of them? It is understandable if you actually feel like bolting from their sight. However, with the understanding you now have that a person with BPD has an illogical thought process, it is imperative that you exercise patience and pay attention to the person letting out their feelings. For one, just having the opportunity to express their deep feelings of anger and dissatisfaction and knowing that someone has heard them loud and clear serves to deflate the ballooned wish to act out. In short, control your frustration and just listen. You will be saving yourself and everyone else around an impending outburst because by having a listening ear, the person's emotions just cool off naturally.

What you may be finding difficult to reconcile at this juncture is your knowledge that the person is telling lies vis-à-vis the position of the person with BPD that their observations are gospel truth. This is where you now need to accept that you are also merely playing out for the sole objective of pre-empting an eruptive episode. What you need to do is show interest while not admitting to anything – neither accepting nor denying.

Here are two ways of achieving this:

Keep mum but show interest

You could give the person your undivided attention as they speak to you pouring out their feelings of dejection and so on, and possibly keep nodding. To further reassure the person that you are paying serious attention, you could throw in some follow up questions derived from exactly what the person said. If, for instance, they feel that people in the family hate them, you may pose a question like: *And when did you begin to feel this way?* Or: *What can you say makes you feel this way?*

While the person may wish to believe that you are swallowing whatever they are saying without a doubt, the truth is that you have not expressed your position in a way to show that you are in agreement.

Quote them

As a relative dealing with someone with BPD, how do you feel when you listen to the person expressing views that you feel are outrageous; like saying how you despise them or how little you think of them? It is understandable if you actually feel like bolting from their sight.

If after every expression of anger or frustration you pick a phrase and interrogate it like you need to understand it better, it shows the person with BPD that they have your full attention. When they tell you the whole family hates them you could pose the question: *So you believe the entire family hates you?* While it may sound ridiculous to your own ears – asking something that you are sure you heard right in the first place – just do it. It serves to show much needed empathy towards the person, and it still keeps you safe from lying to them. You are simply providing the person room to vent out while refraining from endorsing their feelings and views.

People with BPD are plagued with feelings of isolation and loneliness, and that is a fact that relatives need to accept. And once you acknowledge this fact, you do not tire of making a conscious effort of providing attention to the affected persons because you also know that failure to allow them room to speak out their negative feelings only increases chances of them acting out aggressively.

Let everyone participate in the solution

How do you feel when you receive a list of instructions every morning without knowing where your boss is coming from and where they are headed? The reality is that it is not the most motivating way of working. But if you were engaged in analyzing the problem and seeking a solution, you would be glad to know how the decision was reached that you were the most fitting to play the role you are being asked to play. And in that case you would feel obliged to do your best in your role. This is the same thing that people with BPD want.

When you think you have identified the problem with your family member, discuss it in a family forum and seek to know what the affected person feels about it. Then walk the journey of seeking a solution together. Here's the best sequence of events:

- Seek the involvement of the family member with BPD in discussing ways of identifying a solution to the problem already identified

- Seek to know from the affected person if they are in a position to play their particular part of the solution

- Seek to establish if the person requires any assistance from any one or all of the family members and what that assistance is.

You can hope to receive great co-operation from the person with BPD once you involve them all the way in open family discussions. Listening to their views and seeking their participation makes them feel respected. And this is important if you are to expect sincere participation in solving the problem. Do not forget to seek the opinions and readiness to participate from each and every member of the family. Having a person with BPD in the family is actually a family challenge.

<u>Device a plan that every family member can adhere to; a cohesive plan</u>

Do you think that apart from the person with BPD all you other family members are going to agree on everything? No way! Yet that is no reason to frustrate your efforts to bring sanity to your home. So you have to seek ways of working together, trying to recognize what each person feels strong about and how to take everyone's views on board for a common purpose. If tension persists, you can be sure the person with BPD will recognize that and use it to advance the weaknesses you are trying to alleviate.

See what happens, for instance, in a case where a teenager with BPD keeps overindulging and overspending. If the mother is empathetic and keeps bailing out the teenager behind the father's back, and that is simply because the father believes in the teenager keeping to his or her budget, the solution to the teenager's overindulgence and other BPD symptoms will be long in coming. Family members trying to help one of their own who has BPD must, of necessity, work in concert with one another.

Discuss any concerns with the therapist

Does anxiety leave you just because you avoid acknowledging you are anxious? Of course, it doesn't. So you need not fear expressing your concerns to your person's therapist whenever some thought disturbs you. If, for instance, the medication your family member is taking as part of therapy has brought out some negative behaviour, some adverse physical signs, and so on, tell that to the therapist or the doctor concerned. If the person has some history that might interfere with the treatment, or that could help the professional assist better, express it to them. In some of these instances, you just cannot go by the affected member's opinion that you need not speak to the therapist about your concerns.

In fact, you need not fear that you are interfering. If you are expected to be active in the person's recovery process, giving the necessary financial or moral support, how can you then not be allowed to share your anxieties with the professional helping the process? Granted you should not expect the professional to disclose personal matters to you if your family member is above the age of 18yrs, but you break no rules by volunteering helpful information yourself, even when that information touches on the person of your adult family member.

You could frame your question like: Have you noticed so and so has turned obese over this short period of medication? Or: Did you know that our person is a recovering addict of this or that substance? In short, by expressing your fears freely to the therapist, you will be ensuring your family member's life is not endangered and their progress is not inhibited.

Express your expectations

You have gathered as a family to try and help one of you whose mental condition adversely affects everyone in the family. So you are being proactive. Expecting the person you are trying to help to participate proactively is not too much to ask. Experts advise that in communication, you leave no ambiguities as to your expectations. Spell out the role you expect the family member with BPD to play in the adjusting process. Keep it simple by breaking down tasks and specific behaviour. You could, for instance, say: *Keep the volume of the TV in your room at this specific level or below after this hour*. You have clearly stated your expectations as far as some specific behaviour is concerned. Who is to regulate the TV volume? The individual you are trying to assist. And do not succumb to the temptation of adding an ultimatum or a threat to that demand. For example, avoid saying: *Keep the volume of the TV in your room at this specific level or below after this hour* otherwise *I'll take away the TV*.

Once you use threats, you are doing disservice to yourself because then:

- You will be shifting the responsibility to act from the person with BPD to yourself

- You may never make good your threat of taking away the TV even if the person failed to keep his or her side of the bargain. It will therefore be clear to everyone, including the person with BPD, that you were merely expressing empty hostility. Do you think the person will take your demands seriously from then onwards?

Let the person with BPD feel the impact of their actions

Every action has its consequences, and while the actions affect the people around, the people perpetrating the actions should feel the impact of the consequences. When you have people with BPD acting out, possibly trying to harm themselves, they make you walk on eggshells all the time. It also becomes a burden for the family trying to ensure there is someone around them all the time just to monitor the person's behaviour. The reality is that your life ceases to be normal. It may help the situation if you let the person have a taste of that reality when you let other people know your situation.

The person may not wish other people to know that they do act badly and they may feel embarrassed to have their behaviour exposed. If they threaten to commit suicide and you make an emergency call either to medics or to the law enforcement authorities, it can serve as a wake-up call that what the person is doing is serious. They know that an ambulance coming in or police officers calling in cannot be a silent move. That is not something great to be associated with. However, it may be what you need as a family to get this person re-thinking their behaviour of making suicide threats. You need to do whatever is necessary to curb the dangerous behaviour of the person with BPD, which is often not just harmful, but also very costly for the family, both emotionally and financially.

There is an African saying that goes: *You have to undress if you want to bathe.* In your case, you cannot help the person with BPD if, as a family, you fear embarrassment and stigma. If by trying to help you are going to draw the attention of outsiders, let it be. It may be somewhat embarrassing to you all, but it is a necessary helpful move.

Suppose the person becomes enraged on hearing that you are going to call an ambulance owing to their suicide or such other dangerous threat? The answer is get on with it. If you back out, you will be sending a message to that person that they can easily manipulate you. That all they need to do when they have messed up is throw tantrums or behave crazily enraged and you will give in.

Do not withstand abuse

Abuse of any kind; tantrums, threats of causing harm, acts of spitting or even hitting are all abuses you should not tolerate. If you find the threats mild, say like just whining and throwing tantrums, you could decide to walk away. The reason you walk away, besides trying to maintain your sanity of course, is so that you cease to dignify unwarranted tantrums with your attention. If you pay attention to such behaviour, the family member will feel rewarded. And as usual, rewarding bad behaviour is tantamount to encouraging it.

Something else you need to take into account is that by exhibiting aggressive behaviour, whether verbal or physical, the person with BPD may be sending out a message that they need help. Since you are not a medical expert, why not do the necessary and call an ambulance or such other help? You should know that safety is more important than maintaining privacy.

Use threats only as a last resort

Do not use threats or even ultimatums to try and influence the behaviour of the person with BPD. The reason is that you will jeopardize the rehabilitation process if you issue threats and fail to carry them out. If the family member with BPD is undergoing therapy or is seeing a doctor, consult with such a professional before issuing a threat.

Conclusion

Living with a narcissist or a person who has BPD can be extremely difficult. Yet, you've committed yourself to a relationship with that person, so you're ready for the challenges it brings. Now, you have the knowledge about how you can go forward and encourage your loved one to get the help that he or she needs. You must keep in mind that you can act as a support system, but not an enabler. Your job is tough, but now you know how to approach it.

While there may be ups and downs throughout your relationship, you'll find that in time, you and your loved one will learn each other's behavior patterns and can adapt to one another accordingly. If your loved one is committed to seeking help, and you're committed to being there along the way, then you are already well on your way towards improvement. Remember to have patience, avoid taking anything personally as your loved one experiences bad days, and seek outside help when needed. With enough time, healing is possible, and you and your loved one can share a loving, healthy relationship together.

BONUS

CODEPENDENCY

How To Overcome Codependency And Develop Healthy Relationships For Life !

I. Madison

© 2015 Copyright.

Text copyright reserved. I. Madison

The contents of this book may not be reproduced, duplicated or transmitted without direct written permission from the author

Disclaimer : all attempts have been made by the author to provide factual and accurate content. No responsibility will be taken by the author for any damages caused by misuse of the content described in this book. The content of this book has been derived from various sources. Please consult a licensed professional before attempting any techniques outlined in this book.

Table of Contents

Introduction 113
Chapter 1: What is Codependency?....................................... 114

Introduction

Codependency: it's a pattern of behavior that affects an innumerable amount of people, yet, because it falls under the category of "dysfunctional relationships," it's rarely discussed openly. Nonetheless, those living in codependent relationships know that it can be extremely difficult to carry out daily activities and regain a healthy lifestyle. Furthermore, codependency in the U.S. contributes to an overwhelming majority of relationship issues. So, if you're part of a codependent relationship, you're not alone. The bad news about codependency is that codependent behaviors can worsen if the parties involved in the relationship refuse to receive treatment. On the upside, codependents *can* make a recovery and foster a healthy relationship moving forward.

This book will give you the knowledge and tools you'll need to move towards recovery from a codependent relationship. You'll learn how to spot the warning signs of codependency and identify the telling behaviors of codependent individuals. You'll also discover real, applicable methods of coping with codependency so that you can move forward and reestablish healthy relationships. This e-book will outline steps to get your life and relationship in a better place. Enjoy the book, and good luck in your journey toward achieving a healthy, rewarding, and fulfilling relationship.

Chapter 1:
What is Codependency?

Codependency is often defined as a type of behavior in which an individual becomes wholly reliant on another. He or she constantly seeks self-worth based upon another's approval. Oftentimes, one person supports the other individual's undesirable traits or behaviors. This can come in the form of addiction, poor mental health, underachievement, or general lack of self-worth or responsibility. Although codependency typically occurs within romantic relationships, it can also take place across other family dynamics, and can even be found in working, friendly, or community relationships.

In a codependent relationship, one individual seeks constant fulfillment from his or her partner. In some instances, both individuals can become codependent, meaning that both parties are dependent on the fulfillment provided by one another. While this definition in itself may not sound unhealthy, it's important to realize that codependents are problematic because they are unable to achieve a sense of self-worth on their own. They seek validation from others, and cannot establish autonomy by themselves.

Typically, one party in the codependent relationship makes great sacrifices in his or her life in order to put the other person's life first. The individual who routinely makes these sacrifices believes that he or she must continue to appease the other individual, since it has been ingrained in that person's mind that self-worth can be found only through others. This is unhealthy behavior, and can cause serious implications for both parties' mental wellbeing if left untreated.

In many instances, codependents are individuals who tend to support the unhealthy behaviors of their partners. For instance, individuals who pair up with people suffering from borderline personality disorder may be more likely to become codependents. That's because there's a great chance that they'll feel forced to enter into the role of caretaker, which fosters a sense of dependency. The caretaker relies on the sense of validation he or she experiences in being needed by another, and treats the individual who has borderline personality disorder with priority instead of focusing on his or her own life.

Codependents are also commonly partners of narcissists. Sometimes, the codependents in these relationships are referred to as co-narcissists. Narcissists often actively seek and attract individuals that are inclined to putting others' needs before their own. While the codependent relies on making others feel important to achieve a sense of self-worth, the narcissist thrives on that very feeling of importance, which is why codependency is so common within relationships in which narcissists are involved.

As previously mentioned, dysfunctional family relationships are also a different variation of codependency. While children generally must rely on their parents due to the limitations presented by their young age, dysfunctional families flip the roles of the dependents. In other words, children begin to monitor their parents' needs and behaviors. This is typically a result of a parent's (or both parents') unhealthy or destructive behavior towards his or her child.

A parent must take care of him or herself mentally and physically in order to properly care for a child. If he or she is incapable of doing so, a dysfunctional family environment typically arises. The child may become shamed, ignored, or have his or her physical and emotional needs negated by his or her codependent parent. Unfortunately, this scenario usually leads to the passing on of codependent behavior from parent to child, and the child becomes more likely to wind up in a codependent relationship as an adult.

Addiction is also a common source of codependency. Sometimes, one party in the relationship will become an enabler, and the addict's behavior is able to be continued partially due to the fact that the codependent acts in a way that allows it to persist. This is especially common in relationships in which one party is suffering from alcoholism.

While codependency is unfavorable and can be mentally and emotionally taxing on the parties involved, it is something that, once identified, can be treated. Next, we'll examine the signs and symptoms of codependency.

Made in the USA
Lexington, KY
18 February 2016